SOLA SCRIPTURA OR SOLA TRADITIONE?

by

REV. FR. MARK AZIZ, M.Th.

AGORA
UNIVERSITY
PRESS

COPYRIGHT © 2014

Agora University Press

press.agora.edu

ALL RIGHTS RESERVED

No part of this publication may be reproduced, stored in a retrieval system, or transmitted in any form or by any means-electronic, mechanical, graphic, photocopy, recording, taping, information storage, or any other-without written permission of the publisher.

ISBN: 978-0-984891-82-5

HIS HOLINESS **POPE TAWADROS II**
118th *Pope and Patriarch of the great city of Alexandria and the See of St. Mark.*

HIS HOLINESS **PATRIARCH IGNATIUS APHREM II KARIM**
Patriarch of Antioch and All the East.

PRINTED IN THE UNITED STATES OF AMERICA

✟

DEDICATION

THIS BOOK IS DEDICATED WITH LOVE AND AFFECTION TO
SANAA MY WIFE,
AND MY TWO DAUGHTERS VERONIA AND MAKRINA.

CONTENTS

	Acknowledgments	vii
1	Introduction	1
2	Orthodox Patristic Views on Tradition	5
3	The Sources of Revelation in the Medieval Period	49
4	Luther on *Sola Scriptura* and Tradition	94
5	Orthodox and Lutheran in Dialogue	140
6	The Conclusion	170
	Bibliography	186
	About the Author	201

ACKNOWLEDGMENTS

This important work would not have come to fruition without the invaluable help and supervision of Dr. Nick J. Thompson of the Univeristy of Aberdeen. I am grateful for his support and great assistance during the research for this dissertation. I am also indebted to Dr. Darrel Cosden of International Christian College for his encouragement at the beginning of the research.

Thanks are also due to the library staff at International Christian College and 'Queen Margaret' at the University of Aberdeen for allowing me prolonged access to research materials and help in locating information.

Special thanks are due to my blessed wife Sanaa, for her continued sacrifice, support and encouragement. Additionally, I would also like to thank my two daughters Veronia and Makrina for being patient with me during my study.

1 INTRODUCTION

The aim of this book is to investigate the relationship between Scripture and Tradition in the history of the church in the East and the West, and attempt to answer the question whether the Orthodox theology of Tradition have offered a solution to the Reformation debate about theological authority? To address this question, we will examine various questions such as: Why, in the 16th century, did part of the Western church determine there was a conflict between Scripture and Tradition? We will also explore how an Orthodox understanding (or early Western understanding prior to the Great Schism of 1054) of the relationship between Scripture and Tradition might help resolve this perceived conflict, and contribute to the modern dialogue between the Orthodox and Protestant churches, as well as the Protestant and Catholic churches.

To do this, we will start by reviewing the Apostolic Era, passing through the patristic period, and Middle Ages, ultimately culminating in the Reformation. Through this examination we will see how Scripture and Tradition walked hand in hand during the

Patristic era and through Middle Ages. We will also discover the reason for the Great Divorce or 'the division of the Church of England', in the West, and how the principle of *Sola Scriptura* was adopted. Finally, we will examine the discussions between the Orthodox and Lutheran churches, as an example of the unity that can be achieved by discussing the relationship between Tradition and Scripture.

The first chapter of the book will discuss Orthodox Patristic views on Tradition. In it, we will investigate various Orthodox theologians' perspectives on the meaning of Tradition. During this investigation we will examine the concept of the source(s) of revelation throughout the Patristic period. We will then explore through closely defined hermeneutics, the interplay of 'Tradition' and 'traditions' or 'customs'. In doing so we will review the apostolic and patristic approach to Tradition, including the views of early Church Fathers such as Irenaeus, Tertullian, Basil the Great, and Vincent of Lérins, the role of Tradition in Orthodox patristic life and how it relates to Scripture, and illustrate the need for a clear and precise distinction between the Tradition needed for salvation and the local customs that developed in individual parish communities. Ultimately, this chapter will establish how an Orthodox understanding of Tradition would have conceptually and philosophically ameliorated conflicts during the Reformation.

Chapter two will then highlight the sources of Revelation in the Medieval Period. It will specifically examine the perspective of historians including Heiko Oberman and George Tavard. We will then explore the developments of medieval theology emphasizing the late medieval period. Through the work of theologians such as Occam, d'Ailly, Biel, Wessel of Gansfort and Breviscoxa, we will examine the fourteenth century perspective on Tradition, and understand the ultimate confrontation between the nominalists Ockham, Gerson and d'Ailly who supported the idea of Tradition II against Wycliffe, Huss and Gansfort who defended Tradition I contra Tradition II. Additionally, the rise of the so-called heresies against Tradition will be reviewed, highlighting the Wycliffites and the Hussites. Finally, through a comparison of the rift and subsequently reunion attempts between the Oriental and Byzantine Orthodox Churches, on one hand, in contrast with the Great Schism between the Protestant and Western church, which resulted in the innovation of new doctrines, on the other, we will understand how keeping to Tradition is essential for preserving and restoring unity.

In chapter three, we will examine the writings of Luther on *Sola Scriptura* and Tradition which led to the rejection of Tradition and the adoption of the doctrine of *Sola Scriptura* by the Reformers. We will begin by understanding what led Luther towards this adoption through an investigation of the works "The Leipzig disputation" (1519), "On Councils and the Church" (1539), and the historical environment during which they were written. We will comment on these texts through a review of other works by Luther including "The Bondage of the Will" and "The Table-talk". We will ultimately reveal how far Luther's popular ideologies actually conformed the church with the Orthodox Patristic view of Tradition but also how in doing so, he opened the door for other reformers to stray away from the one true Tradition.

Chapter four will discuss the dialogue between the Orthodox and Lutheran churches by investigating Melanchthon, the true author of the *Augsburg Confession* and one of Luther's main Patristic scholars. The Greek version of the *Augsburg Confession* was the key that started the dialogue between the different churches in the West during the middle of the sixteenth century. This Chapter concludes with a review of the agreed upon statements and plenaries concerned with Scripture and Tradition upon the resuming of the dialogue at the end of the twentieth century.

The concluding chapter of the book will summarize the debate between Scripture and Tradition and explain how the new approach could be *Sola Traditione* rather than *Sola Scriptura*. Additionally, it will attempt to show potential benefits and pitfalls of the current ecclesial dialogues on the topic and it will try to offer some recommendations for future dialogues.

2 ORTHODOX PATRISTIC VIEWS ON TRADITION

Before we can discover how the Orthodox Patristic Tradition could help in the debate between Scripture and Tradition during the Pre-reformation period, we must determine first what the Orthodox Patristic Tradition is. The word tradition can mean different things, and there is a distinction to be made between the universal Tradition, the source of revelation, and particular traditions or local church customs. To determine the differences and distinctions, we will explore the Orthodox Patristic view and show that Scripture was the first written part of Tradition. We will also explore and expand on (1) the nature of extra-scriptural teaching included in the Tradition of the Apostolic Era, which was widely accepted by all churches at that time; (2) the importance of Tradition for both theories regarding the authorship of the gospels including, the older view that assumes eyewitnesses wrote the gospels and the more modern view that finds they were written at a later stage. We will use this information along with a review of the Early Church Fathers including Irenaeus, Tertullian, St. Basil and St. Vincent of Lérins, to determine the role and authority of Tradition in the Patristic era. This will give us a comprehensive understanding of the definition of the Orthodox Patristic Tradition in the Church and allow us to determine how Tradition can accept extra-biblical teachings, as well as how this Patristic understanding could have positively contributed to both the Pre-reformation debate and current dialogues.

Defining Tradition

The New International Dictionary of the Christian Church defines "tradition", or the Greek word *paradosis,* as handing something over, or a teaching which has been handed down.[1] *"Paradosis"* occurs thirteen times in the New Testament, including eight times in the Gospel of Matthew Chapter 7 and Mark Chapter 15 where we find the Lord rebuking the Jews for forsaking the Commandments and keeping their fathers' traditions.[2] St. Paul also uses *"paradosis"* to describe the old traditions and customs of the Jews and the Gentiles[3], and again to describe what he taught the Churches by words or by letters.[4] At one point St. Paul instructs the Thessalonians Church to: "Stand firm, then, brothers, and keep the traditions that we taught you, whether by word of mouth or by

---

[1] J. Douglas, *The New International Dictionary of the Christian Church*, (Exeter: The Paternoster Press, 1974), 982. (The term "tradition" comes from the Latin *traditio,* but the Greek word *paradidomi* from which *paradosis* "tradition" is derived, means "to hand something over". The New Testament employs the verb in a variety of ways (Matt. 11:27; Acts 14:26; 1Pet. 2:23), but the noun is reserved for teaching which has been handed down. Apostolic teaching-which included facts about Christ, their theological importance, and their ethical implications for Christian living- was described as tradition (I Cr. 11:2; II Thess. 2:15) It had divine sanction (I Cr. 11:23; Gal.1:11-16) and once committed to writing was to be preserved by the church (Jude 3; 2 Tim. 1:13; Rom 6:17). Jesus rejected tradition, but only in the sense of human accretion lacking divine sanction (Mark 7:3-9)).
[2] Matthew 15:2, 15:3 and 15:6; Mark 7:3,7:5,7:8,7:9 and 7:13.
[3] Gal. 1:14 and Col. 2:8.
[4] I Cr. 11:2, II Th. 2:15 and II Th. 3:3.

letter".⁵ This verse constitutes a very loose definition and understanding of "tradition". This is largely due to the potential confusion that could arise by asking whether these traditions would include the teachings of the Jews which Jesus disapproved? Therefore, we must look for additional sources to further refine this definition.

Paradosis is the very life of the Holy Trinity as it has been revealed by Christ Himself and testified by the Holy Spirit.⁶ Lossky elaborates:

> Tradition in its primary notion is not the revealed content, but the unique mode of receiving revelation, a faculty owed to the Holy Spirit, who renders the Church capable of knowing the Incarnate Word in His relationship with the Father [supreme gnosis which is, for the Fathers of the first centuries, Theology in the proper meaning of the word] as well as the mysteries of the divine economy, from the creation of heaven and earth of Genesis to the new heaven and new earth of the Apocalypse.⁷

Bishop Ware expounds on the Orthodox Christian Tradition stating:

> Christian Tradition, in this case, is the faith which Jesus Christ imparted to the Apostles, and which since the Apostles' time has been handed down

---

⁵ II Thess. 2:15.
⁶ G. Debis, *Tradition in the Orthodox Church*. Available [Internet] <http://www.goarch.org/ourfaith/articles7116.asp> [9th October 2002]
⁷ Erickson John, Bird Thomas, eds., *Vladimir Lossky: In the Image and Likeness of God*, (London & Oxford: Mowbrays, 1974), 154-156.

from generation to generation in the Church. But to Orthodox Christians, Tradition means something more concrete and specific than this. It means the books of the Bible; it means the creed; it means the decrees of the ecumenical councils and the Writings of the Fathers; it means the Canons, the Service books, the Holy Icons- in fact the whole system of the Doctrine.[8]

However, not everything received from the past is of equal value, nor is everything received from the past necessarily true.[9] Ware explains that the decrees of Jassy[10] do not stand at the same level as the Nicene Creed, nor the writings of Athanasius occupy the same position as the Gospel of St. John.[11] He quotes the Council of Carthage in 257: "The Lord said I am the Truth; He did not say I am custom." Here Ware, in his definition, posits that Tradition is as old as the Apostles, held by everyone in all generations since their time, and in every part of the world by all churches. Although Ware does not accept as infallible everything handed down from the past, he offers no criteria to distinguish between what is true and untrue, or between things of high importance and low importance.

Fr. Malaty confirms that Tradition essentially is 'Unity with Christ' through the Holy Spirit.[12] He sees that the act of transmission of truth is realized not only by the Apostles' writings

---

[8] Timothy Ware, *The Orthodox Church*, (England: Penguin Books, 1983), 204.
[9] Ibid., 205.
[10] A local council held in Romania (1642).
[11] Ibid, 205.
[12] T. Malaty, *The Orthodox Concept: Tradition and Orthodoxy*, (Alexandria: St. George Church, 1979), 8.

but more so by the Holy Spirit who guided them and gave them new life which is 'life in Christ'.[13] So, the action of the Holy Spirit is to maintain the "Tradition of Christ" in the church through successive generations, as He always lives and acts in the church and not in mechanical repetition of the past.[14] In other words, Tradition is the living stream of the one life of the Church which brings up the past with all its aspects as a *living present*, and extends the present towards the morrow without deformations.[15] Malaty provides that Tradition is a dynamic act transforming the Church into its eternal form experiencing the past, present and future at the same time through Tradition.

The *Didache* is perhaps the first document written after the books of the New Testament – written circa the end of the first century or in the first quarter of the second century – which links the Scripture with the writings of the Patristic period. It includes precepts of morality, organizational issues, liturgical functions, and simple dogmatic pronouncements, where it shows the liturgical unity of the Apostolic era. Debis states that although St. Athanasius did not canonize the *Didache* as part of the New Testament, he allowed catechumens to read it for their instruction.[16] This affirms the Orthodox understanding that the New Testament was written in the first century according to the Orthodox Tradition, in

---

[13] Ibid.
[14] F.F. Bruce, *Tradition Old and New*, (Exeter Devon: The Paternoster Press, 1970), 20-21.
[15] Malaty, 8.
[16] George Debis, "The Concept of Tradition In The Fathers Of The Church", *Greek Orthodox Theological Churches Review*, 15, no.1 (Spring 1970): 31.

contrast with the twentieth century Western debate around when the New Testament was written, discussed further below.

Among other aspects, the *Didache* teaches that the believer should seek out day by day the faces of the saints, in order that they may rest upon their words.[17] It also lists instructions for what are believed to be the earliest baptismal preparations and baptismal rites.[18] Chapter eight of the *Didache* is one of the oldest writings instructing to move the days of fasting away from those celebrated by the Jews—the second and the fifth days of the week—to the days Orthodox Christians currently fast, the fourth day and the day of Preparation (Friday). Additionally, chapter nine is one of the earliest institutional records of the Eucharistic assembly, which includes instructions that the non-baptized should not partake of the communion. Chapter ten outlines the prayer said at the conclusion of the communion, which with minor variations is still used by Orthodox Christians today. Finally, chapter fourteen formulates the assembly on the Lord's Day:

> But every Lord's day gather yourselves together, and break bread, and give thanksgiving after having confessed your transgressions, that your sacrifice may be pure. But let no one who is at odds with his fellow come together with you, until they be reconciled, that your sacrifice may not be profaned. For this is that which was spoken by the Lord: 'In every place and time offer to me a pure

---

[17] The *Didache*, IV.
[18] The *Didache*, VII.

sacrifice; for I am a great King, says the Lord, and my name is wonderful among the nations.'[19]

The epistle of St. Clement, the Bishop of Rome, to the Corinthians is generally considered the earliest Patristic writing. In it St. Clement outlines the Patristic principle of Tradition to support his urging the church to preserve the ministerial orders appointed by the Lord and clarifies the ordinances of the apostles, that there might be no contention respecting the priestly office saying:

> The apostles have preached the Gospel to us from the Lord Jesus Christ; Jesus Christ has done so from God. Christ therefore was sent forth by God, and the apostles by Christ. Both these appointments, then, were made in an orderly way, according to the will of God. Having therefore received their orders, and being fully assured by the resurrection of our Lord Jesus Christ, and established in the word of God, with full assurance of the Holy Ghost, they went forth proclaiming that the kingdom of God was at hand. And thus preaching through countries and cities, they appointed the first-fruits [of their labours], having first proved them by the Spirit, to be bishops and deacons of those who should afterwards believe. Nor was this any new thing, since indeed many ages before it was written concerning bishops and deacons. For thus says the Scripture in a certain place, 'I will appoint their bishops in righteousness, and their deacons in

---

[19] *Didache, or Teaching of the Twelve Apostles*, trans. by Roberts Donaldson. Available [Internet] <http://www.earlychristianwritings.com/text/didache-roberts.html> [3rd March 2004].

faith.'[20]

According to Tavard, the Early Patristic Church viewed Tradition as the art of handing on the Gospel, not in a way that was separated from the good news of Christ, but as the power of the Gospel itself. This understanding inspires the devotion and the loyalty of the Church in preserving and handing down the good news, because Tradition emerges from the Gospel.[21] He observes:

> If one likes to see the Revelation and its way of approach to us on a horizontal plane, the sequence, Word-written Gospel-Tradition, seems to be most adequate. Yet this is not to be understood in terms of substitution. Tradition is no substitute for the Gospel. The Gospel does not replace the Living Word. The Word is the presence that is experienced when we read the Gospel in the books that the Church has preserved.[22]

Debis partially concurs with the judgment of Tavard, agreeing that there is no chasm between Biblical studies and the Patristic Tradition; both are cumulative experiences of the Church united in Christ and led by the Spirit towards the fulfilment of the eschaton. He asserts that the Fathers exercised their hermeneutics and teachings as instruments of the Holy Spirit and as a perpetual

---

[20] Clement of Rome, *Letter of Clement To The Corinthians*, trans. by Roberts Donaldson. Available [Internet] < http://www.earlychristianwritings.com/text/1clement-roberts.html> [3rd March 2004].
[21] George Tavard, *Holy Writ Or Holy Church, The Crisis Of the Protestant Reformation*, (London: Burns & Oats, 1959), 3.
[22] Ibid, 4.

witness to the unceasing presence of the Holy Spirit stating:

> One point, however, must be made clear, and that is that we cannot study the Scripture without the Fathers of the Church. *sola scriptura* or *sola traditio* have no place in the scheme of the Orthodox Theology. 'Scripture and Fathers' are referred to and quoted together, because Scripture could not be studied and interpreted without the Fathers. There is no doubt that the Fathers were the great exegetes and interpreters of Scripture and it is most significant that almost all the Fathers wrote and preached on the Bible. They were 'The eyes of the Church' and used all the hermeneutical principles and methods so that they might convey the biblical message of salvation to their fellow men. Such being the case, it is right to say that 'Scripture without interpretation is not Scripture at all; the moment it is used and becomes alive it is always interpreted Scripture.'[23]

Tradition & Traditions

For a long time the distinction between 'Tradition' and 'traditions' has been debated. Some theologians accepted a distinction between the two while others did not. For example, Bishop Aghiorgoussis of Pittsburgh states:

> A favourite distinction among theologians is the one between Tradition and traditions. Tradition, with a capital T, is the life of the Spirit of the Church. It is this life that makes the continuity of Truth and Life in the Church, and gives to it its stability, continuity, and unchangeability. While traditions (with small t) are the concrete and

---
[23] Debis, *The Concept of Tradition In The Fathers Of The Church*, 27-8.

historic manifestation of that Tradition, they may change. As in the Bible one distinguishes between the letter and the spirit, so in the tradition of the church in general one distinguishes between the context and its expression.[24]

Debis, in the words of a contemporary theologian Professor Konstaninides, introduces a similar principle in a more sophisticated way.

> Contemporary Orthodox theologians have suggested that in order to understand more fully the concept or the doctrine of the Patristic Tradition in particular or the concept of Tradition in general we might speak of Tradition [with capital T] and about traditions [with small t]. It has been suggested that the whole historical scheme of Tradition should be described as follows: tradition [with small t] which is the oral transmission of the Divine revelation which precedes the Scripture; then Scripture [with Capital S], the scripture [with small s] which include all the forms of the written expressions, interpretation and formulation of the received Truth; and finally Tradition [with capital T] which the Apostolic and Ecclesiastical Tradition and is absolutely necessary for the salvation of mankind.[25]

He then cautions us that this distinction is misleading, because both Tradition and traditions are integral parts of the life of the Church expressing the totality of the Christian way of life

---

[24] M. Aghiorgoussis, *The Dogmatic Tradition of the Orthodox Church*. Available [Internet] <http://paul.goarch.org/en/ourfaith/articles/article8038.asp> [2nd October 2002].
[25] Debis, *The Concept Of The Tradition In The Fathers Of The Church*, 41.

that leads to Salvation. He gives examples of necessary Traditional doctrines, including the Incarnation, the historical truth of crucifixion and resurrection, the Eucharist, the sign of the cross and the threefold immersion in the baptismal font. He cites St. John Chrysostom[26] and St. Photius to confirm that there is a line that can be drawn between ecclesiastical faith (Tradition), whose rejection leads to death, and the ecclesiastical customs (traditions) that differ from place to place. Irenaeus, agreeing with Photius, rejects Pope Victor's plan to excommunicate Asian Churches for not holding Roman customs, apropos Easter and Fasting.[27]

Bishop Ware insists on the difference between the Tradition and traditions in a more emphatic way. He argues that many traditions (customs) that have been handed down are human and accidental—pious opinions—but not a true part of the one Tradition, the essential Christian message.[28] This does not show a disagreement between Orthodox theologians, but it shows a longing for a clearer definition of the particularities of the understanding of Tradition needed for salvation.

Here we can sense a real tension between Ware and Debis. Ware insists that some traditions are human and not a true part of Tradition, leaving the distinction ambiguous without offering any criteria to point towards 'false' or 'non-essential' parts

---

[26] Debis, *Tradition in the Orthodox Church*.[Internet] ("It is Tradition, seek no more.").
[27] Debis, *The Concept Of Tradition In The Fathers Of The Church*, 42.
[28] Ware, *The Orthodox Church*, 205.

of Tradition. In contrast Debis, in an extreme manner, cautions that all Tradition and traditions lead to salvation. Here some questions pose themselves. First, in the case of possible mishandlings of the Tradition arising within the Church, how should the Church or a parishioner recognize and deal with them? The conditions of discernment given by St. Vincent of Lérins provide the best answer.[29] St. Vincent posits three conditions for doctrines to be held in the Church. He says that doctrines should be held always, everywhere, and by all. The authority to judge will vary. Sometimes the judge will have to be the clergy (priest or bishop) if the mishandling arises within the local Church. In other situations, it will need either a local, or an ecumenical council to consider the potential abuses or the heresies and adjudicate action properly.

The Orthodox theologian would argue that ecumenical councils (e.g. the first seven councils of the undivided church) could not make mistakes. This is partly because Jesus promised to be with the Church to the end of time[30] and to send the Holy Spirit to guide it in the truth forever[31]. Additionally, the Orthodox (and Catholics) validate these ecumenical Councils because they are a gathering of bishops who were successors to the apostles from all over the world. The Reformers, perhaps because they were subject

---

[29] I will discuss his reception and understanding of Tradition in detail later in this chapter.
[30] Matthew 28:20.
[31] John 14:16.

to additional Catholic "ecumenical" councils (e.g. Lateran IV in 1215 or the Council of Florence in 1439), argued that even ecumenical councils could make mistakes.

The Sources of Revelation in the Early Church

Oberman in his book, *The Dawn of the Reformation*, rejects a simple clash of 'Scripture and Tradition' in favor of a tension between two concepts of tradition: Tradition I and Tradition II. He begins by going back to the Patristic fathers in search of the precise content and connotation of the sources of revelation.[32] If we look to Oberman's analysis of the understanding of Tradition in the eyes of the forerunners of the Reformers, we see that he calls the single exegetical tradition of the interpreted scripture 'Tradition I.' This, in his view, is acceptable to Protestantism in so far as it represented the Church's historical cumulative attempt to interpret the Scripture with the condition it would always have to derive its authority from Scripture alone and not from any unwritten tradition or apostolic succession. The two source theory, which allows for an extra-biblical oral tradition 'Tradition II,' implies the insufficiency of Scripture, which necessarily means that there is an essential part of salvation written and kept within the tradition.[33] If we do as Oberman advocates, we see that from the beginning, the Patristic fathers saw revelation in terms of one source—Tradition:

---

[32] Ibid, 270.
[33] Heiko Oberman, *The Dawn of the Reformation: Essays in Late Medieval and Early Reformation thought*, (Edinburgh: T& T. Clark LTD, 1986), 373-381.

In the final analysis, however, when we say that the Church possesses and preserves Revelation we mean to say that she does this because the Revelation is Tradition *(paradosis)* and becomes Tradition within the Church. It is tradition precisely because it was transmitted *(paradothe)* in Christ and in the Holy Spirit, and it becomes Tradition because the Church preserves it through the course of the history, as the power of life. In other words, Tradition is the unceasing existence of Revelation in the Church.[34]

Bishop Ware notes that the Bible forms a part of the Tradition, and sometimes Tradition is defined as 'The Oral teaching of Christ, not recorded in writing by his immediate disciples." He notes that not only non-Orthodox but even many Orthodox writers have adapted this way of treating Scripture and Tradition as two different sources of Revelation. Ultimately, he explains that there is only one source of Revelation –Tradition; because Scripture exists within Tradition and to separate them or contrast the two is to weaken the idea of both.[35]

The Early Church Fathers considered Scripture and Tradition an unbroken whole, one contained within the other. They found harmony between the spoken word and Scripture.[36] St. John Chrysostom in his fourth homily on second Thessalonians explained verse 2:15 saying:

---

[34] Paradosis Scouteris, "The Orthodox Understanding of Tradition", *Sobornost - Eastern Churches Review*, Vol.4, No. 1, (1982): 32.
[35] Ware, *The Orthodox Church*, 205.
[36] Scouteris, 36.

> Hence it is manifest, that they did not deliver all things by Epistle, but many things also unwritten, and in like manner both the one and the other are worthy of credit. Therefore let us think the Tradition of the Church also worthy of Credit, It is Tradition, seek no farther. [37]

Other theologians interpret this quotation as a classic example for extra-biblical teachings only.

Ware finds there are six different outward expressions of Tradition, which is the source of the Orthodox faith. First there is Scripture, which is not set up over the church but is something living and understood within and by the church. Second, there are the seven ecumenical councils, which are infallible and constitute an abiding and irrevocable authority alongside Scripture. After the seventh council, he observes that the Orthodox Church used two chief ways of expressing its mind: local councils and letters and statements of faith put out by individual bishops, both of which are liable to error.[38] Third, Ware notes the importance of the early church fathers and the application of their exegesis in the life of the Orthodox Church, and notes that according to Orthodox Tradition there is no end to the age of the fathers. Fourth is the Liturgy, where church life preserves and proclaims its faith day by day. Fifth are the canon laws, which were collected by St. Nicodemus of the Holy Mountain and published in 1800. Last are Icons, as they are

---

[37] John Chrysostom, *Homilies on Thessalonians* in Philip Schaff, eds., *Nicene and Post Nicene Fathers*, First Series, 14 v. (Edinburgh: T& T Clark, reprint 1994), 8:390.
[38] CITE. He also notes that there have been 13 Orthodox doctrinal statements put out by individuals since 787. Ware, *The Orthodox Church,* 211.

one of the ways whereby God is revealed to man.[39] In summary:

> Such are the primary elements which form an outward point of view and make up the Tradition of the Orthodox Church – Scripture, Councils, Fathers, Liturgy, Canons, and Icons. These things are not to be separated and contrasted, for it is the same Holy Spirit which speaks through them all, and together they make up a single whole, each part being understood in the light of the rest.[40]

Here we can see that the Early Church adhered to Tradition in its full meaning where Tradition includes: Scripture, its exposition, oral traditions, liturgies, prayers and more extra-biblical teachings. All such extra-biblical teachings were used without biblical warrants and with no contradictions to Scripture. Some of these parts of the extra-biblical teachings were universal and apostolic like the triple immersions in the baptismal font, while some others were local such as the wording and the choice of certain scriptural readings for different liturgical prayers.

The Apostolic Tradition

F.F. Bruce outlines three main elements in his examination of Paul's references to the Tradition of Christ. First is a summary of the Christian message uttered as a declaration of faith with particular emphasis on the death and the resurrection of Christ. Secondly, he points out the various deeds and the words of Christ and in particular those that declare the origins of the Eucharist.

---

[39] Ibid, 207-214.
[40] Ibid, 214-215.

Finally, there are the ethical and procedural rules of Christians.[41]

The apostles revealed that one of the sources of the authority for their apostolate is the Tradition they had received through their discipleship of the Lord, so they preached as eyewitnesses to the events of Christ's life and his saving acts.[42] Many references in the New Testament affirm this authority such as I John 1:1, John 19:35, Luke 1:2, and II Peter 1:16-19. Furthermore, when the eleven apostles decided to appoint another disciple to replace Judas, they established only one condition; that he should have accompanied them during the Lord's ministry from the time of the Lord's baptism. This one was called to be as an eyewitness to the resurrection of the Lord as stated in Acts 1:21-22. Fr. Malaty summarizes the apostolic tradition saying:

> In Brief, we can say that the church in the apostolic age accepted the living Tradition, by which she received the books of the Old testament, conceived its prophecies, discovered its types and symbols, acknowledged its unity with the apostolic testimony, received the witnesses of the apostles, declared the authority of their successors in preserving the Christian faith and practiced the true worship of God.[43]

Schaff argues that the four gospels have their common source in the personal interaction of writers (Matthew and John) with Christ, and the apostolic oral tradition and some other

---

[41] Bruce, 29-33.
[42] Malaty, 10.
[43] Ibid, 13.

eyewitnesses (Mark and Luke). He adds, they did not create a divine image of Jesus, but rather preserved and re-produced it in time. The gospel story was being constantly repeated in public preaching and private discussions. He gives the example of Luke who used, according to his own statement, oral tradition as well as written documents on certain parts of the life of Jesus, which doubtless emerged early among the first disciples.[44] In this regard he notes:

> The only certain basis for the solution of the problem is given to us in the preface of Luke. He mentions two sources of his own Gospel—but not necessarily of the two other synoptic Gospels—namely, the oral tradition or deliverance of original "eyewitnesses and ministers of the word" (apostles, evangelists, and other primitive disciples), and a number of written "narratives," drawn up by "many," but evidently incomplete and fragmentary, so as to induce him to prepare, after accurate investigation, a regular history of "those matters which have been fulfilled among us." Besides this important hint, we may be aided by the well-known statements of Papias about the Hebrew Gospel of Matthew and the Greek Mark, whom he represents as the interpreter. The chief and common source from which the Synoptists derived their Gospels was undoubtedly the living apostolic tradition or teaching which is mentioned by Luke in the first order. This teaching was nothing more or less than a faithful report of the words and deeds of Christ himself by honest and intelligent eyewitnesses. He told his disciples to

---

[44] Schaff Philip, *History of The Christian Church*, 8 v., 1:431 [CD- ROM]: The Master Christian Library, Version 6, Ages Software digital Library, USA: Albany, 1998.

preach, not to write, the gospel, although the writing was, of course, not forbidden, but became necessary for the preservation of the gospel in its purity. They had at first only "hearers;" while the law and the prophets had readers.[45]

However, most modern scholars reject the basic belief of the earlier Christians that the Gospels were written by eyewitnesses.

Ehrman avers that most modern scholars have come to accept the "four-source hypothesis" explanation as the least problematic theory for the synoptic Gospels:

> According to this hypothesis, Mark was the first Gospel to be written. It was used by both Matthew and Luke. In addition, both of these other Gospels had access to another source, called Q (from the German word for "source", Quelle). Q provided Matthew and Luke with the stories that they have in common that are not, however, found in Mark. Moreover, Matthew had a source (or group of sources) of his own, from which he drew stories found in neither of the other Gospels. Scholars have simply labeled this source (or sources) M (for Matthew's special source). Likewise, Luke had a source (or group of sources) for stories that he alone tells; not surprisingly, this is called L (Luke's special source). Hence, according to this hypothesis, four sources lie behind our three Synoptic Gospels: Mark, Q, M, and L. The cornerstone of this hypothesis is the theory that Matthew and Luke both used Mark.[46]

---

[45] Ibid, 485.
[46] Bart Ehrman, *The New Testament: A Historical Introduction To The Early Christian Writings*, (New York, Oxford: Oxford University Press, reprint 1997), 73

However, neither Schaff nor Ehrman's view of sources miss the Orthodox principle of Tradition. We shall have two ways to discuss the possibilities of 'gospel writing' addressed above. The first is by what might appear to modern scholars like Schaff as 'out of date'. The second is using possibilities outlined in modern times by scholars like Ehrman. The first possibility is that eyewitnesses wrote the Gospels within fifteen to sixty years from the date of the resurrection of Christ. This means that the Gospel content was kept in the Church for a certain period within Tradition until it was recorded. The second possibility is that they were written later and referred to older available sources at that time. This second possibility confirms the same principle in a more emphatic way. It means that the message of the Gospels was kept for a longer time within Tradition before it was written down. Subsequently, these presupposed older sources should be considered as part of Tradition.

Tradition According to Irenaeus[47]

Fr. Malaty in his analysis of Irenaeus – who is known as the "the Father of the Ecclesiastical Tradition"[48] – summarized Irenaeus' thought about the Tradition in four main points. First, Irenaeus considers that Tradition, which derives from the apostles, is assured by the uninterrupted succession of church bishops.

---

[47] Irenaeus (c.175-c.195) bishop of Lyons, see Douglas, 516
[48] Malaty, 22

Secondly, the Holy Spirit, who vivifies the life of the church every day, keeps Tradition unblemished. Thirdly, Tradition is not exclusive but is freely available to all who wish to accept the truth in every church all over the world. Finally, he found the heretics' use of the same Scriptures (but misinterpreting them, although they were read within the church) was inconsistent with the Tradition of the apostles.[49] Clapsis quotes Irenaeus to confirm this saying:

> But he who is acquainted with the Homeric writings will recognize the verses indeed, but not the subject to which they are applied... But if he takes them and restores each of them to its proper position, he at once destroys the narrative in question. In like manner he also who retains unchangeable in his heart the rule of truth which he received by means of baptism, will doubtless recognize the names, the expressions, and the parables taken from the Scripture, but will by no means acknowledge the blasphemous use which these men make of them. For though he will acknowledge the gems, he will certainly not receive the fox instead of the likeness of the king. But when he has restored every one of the expressions quoted to its proper positions, and has fitted it to the body of the truth, he will lay bare, and prove to be without any foundation, the figment of these heretics.[50]

In describing the unity of the faith of the church throughout the whole world, Irenaeus states:

---

[49] Ibid, 22
[50] Emmanuel Clapsis, *Orthodoxy in Conversation: Orthodox Ecumenical Engagements*, (Brookline: Holy Cross Orthodox Press, 2000), 23.

As I have already observed, the Church, having received this preaching and this faith, although scattered throughout the whole world, yet, as if occupying but one house, carefully preserves it. She also believes these points [of doctrine] just as if she had but one soul, and one and the same heart, and she proclaims them...For although the languages of the world are dissimilar, yet the import of the tradition is one and the same. For churches which have been planted in Germany do not believe or hand down anything different, nor do those in Spain, nor those in Gaul, nor those in the East, nor those in Egypt, nor those in Libya, nor those which have been established in the central regions of the world.[51]

Florovsky uses this Irenaean excerpt to show that the Gnostics re-arranged the Scriptural evidence in a pattern that is quite alien to Scripture itself.[52] Debis adds that Irenaeus has established a strong link between Scripture and Tradition by pointing to the essential need for historical continuity and by showing that subjective interpretations of Scripture are sins implicating man's own self, disrespecting the Holy Trinity, and rejecting one's personal salvation. He says: "Tradition, therefore, in the eyes of St. Irenaeus has a profound soteriological meaning and those who violate its principles are bound to eternal punishment".[53]

---

[51] Irenaeus, *Against Heresies Book I*, Ch. X, in Alexander Roberts and James Donaldson, eds, *Ante- Nicene Fathers*, 10 V. (T& T Clark, Edinburgh, reprint 1996), 1:331.
[52] George Florovsky, *Bible, Church, Tradition: An Eastern Orthodox View*, in Richard Haugh eds. *Volume One in The Collected Works of George Florovsky*, (Vanduz, Europe: Büchervertriebsanstalt, 1987), 78.
[53] Debis, *The Concept Of Tradition In The Fathers Of The Church*, 44.

Whenever the expression 'oral Tradition' is used this does not mean it is still oral. It means it was orally handed down from Christ himself or the apostles and then written somewhere at certain time either in liturgies, epistles, books (not canonized), or in other forms. St. Irenaeus gives the warrant to the true Tradition through the four main criteria (previously explained). However, he did not offer a solution in the case where the Church itself would err. This ultimately shows the strong belief of the Early Church Fathers in the infallibility of the Church, provided that the Holy Spirit is the leader and the guide at all times. This is the main character in the Patristic Church, its infallibility (Eph. 5:25-27) and the continuous presence of the Holy Spirit.

Oberman argues that, for Irenaeus, Episcopal succession does not constitute a channel of oral tradition that would stand alongside Scripture as a second source of revelation. Rather, this is the task of all of us, having received what was first given by the successors via the Church Fathers, to preserve the rule of faith from the first *kerygma* to the church, and reversibly, to enable the church to trace this *kerygma* back through the Church Fathers to the apostles.[54] Clapsis, in his examination of Irenaeus, realizes that Tradition refers not only to Christ and early apostolic faith, but also includes the way the church—always in its catholicity—reads, interprets, re-presents and re-activates the subject of divine revelation in its life. He therefore explains 'the rule of faith' as the

---

[54] Oberman, *The Dawn of the Reformation*, 273.

faith in the Trinity and all salvific economies carried out by Jesus Christ up to the final accomplishment.[55]

The arguments of Oberman have no traction with those of Irenaeus. Irenaeus puts the Episcopal succession as an assurance for keeping the true Tradition without interruption. This does not mean that 'Episcopal succession would innovate a new doctrine or constitute a second source of revelation through its oral teachings'. Thus, the apostolic succession works as a guardian of the extra-biblical teachings, which include teachings written in non-canonized books such as *Didache*, liturgies, etcetera.

Tradition According to Tertullian[56]

Tertullian's approach does not differ from Irenaeus significantly. Malaty summarizes his approach in four main ideas. The core idea is that there is no secret Tradition; rather it is well known to the church. Secondly, he found that the surest test of the authenticity of doctrine is that the churches had been founded by and were continuously linked to the apostles. Thirdly, he illustrated that oral tradition or the "rule of faith" *(regula fidei)* is the key to the correct exegesis of Scripture; a rule which the heretics have disregarded. Finally, he mentions that Tradition was passed down through the practice of worship.[57]

---

[55] Clapsis, 24.
[56] Tertullian (c.160/70-c.215/20) African moralist, apologist and theologian, see Douglas, 960.
[57] Malaty, 23.

The third point (above) parallels Tradition I in Oberman's terms, while the fourth point represents Tradition II. So, if we trust the Church to preserve Scripture and its expositions, we should therefore also trust her to keep the extra-scriptural teaching as well. Otherwise, we cannot trust her to preserve either of them.

Tertullian affirms that some elements of Tradition connected to baptism, Eucharist, offering for the dead, fasting and kneeling on the Lord's Day and the forehead signing of the cross are observed in the church with no biblical warrant but were received from the apostles:

> If, for these and other such rules, you insist upon having positive Scripture injunction, you will find none. Tradition will be held forth to you as the originator of them, custom as their strengthener, and faith as their observer. That reason will support tradition, and custom, and faith, you will either yourself preserve, or learn from someone else. These instances therefore will make it sufficiently plain that you can vindicate the keeping of even unwritten tradition established by custom, the proper witness for tradition when demonstrated by long continued observance.[58]

Contrary to what Oberman observed, a closer look at Tertullian would show that he opposes any notion that there is a source of revelation in addition to the writings of the Apostles, undermining

---

[58] Tertullian, *The Chaplet or De Corona*, Ch. I, in Alexander Roberts and James Donaldson, eds. *Ante Nicene Fathers*, 10 v. (Edinburgh: T& T Clark, reprint 1997), 3: 94,95.

the sufficiency of the Holy Scriptures.[59] Tertullian explains that there is only one source of revelation, that which is Tradition, and the Scripture is an integral part within it. In other words, he acknowledged that Tradition covers everything including the Scriptures, and all sufficiency lies there. Tertullian, in the twenty first chapter of his treatise *Prescription Against Heretics*, asserts that all doctrines are true, provided that they come through the Church of the Apostles, as taught by God through Christ. Concerning all other opinions with no such divine origin and apostolic Tradition for support, he says:

> From this, therefore, do we draw up our rule? Since the Lord Jesus Christ sent the apostles to preach, (our rule is) that no others ought to be received as preachers than those whom Christ appointed; for "no man knoweth the Father save the Son, and he to whomsoever the Son will reveal Him." Nor does the Son seem to have revealed Him to any other than the apostles, whom He sent forth to preach -that, of course, which He revealed to them. Now, what that was which they preached -in other words, what it was which Christ revealed to them -can, as I must here likewise prescribe, properly be proved in no other way than by those very churches which the apostles founded in person, by declaring the gospel to them directly themselves, both vivâ voce, as the phrase is, and subsequently by their epistles. If, then, these things are so, it is in the same degree manifest that all doctrine which agrees with the apostolic churches -those molds and original sources of the faith must be reckoned

---

[59] Oberman, *The Dawn of the Reformation*, 275.

for truth, as undoubtedly containing that which the (said) churches received from the apostles, the apostles from Christ, Christ from God. Whereas all doctrine must be prejudged as false which savors of contrariety to the truth of the churches and apostles of Christ and God. It remains, then, that we demonstrate whether this doctrine of ours, of which we have now given the rule, has its origin in the tradition of the apostles, and whether all other doctrines do not ipso facto proceed from falsehood. We hold communion with the apostolic churches because our doctrine is in no respect different from theirs. This is our witness of truth. [60]

This quote underlines the truth, that, only what is handed down from the apostles and preserved from generation to generation without any interruption is the necessary condition for accepting any articles of Tradition. This gives the Church the authority to condemn heretics who tried to deviate from this rule, either by innovating new articles in the Tradition or misinterpreting Scripture.

Tradition according to St. Basil[61]

Fr. Malaty states that St. Basil is mentioned by other Fathers many times because of his writings as an honest witness of the true Orthodox Faith. St. Basil regards oral tradition as a guide for the true interpretation of Scriptures, which heretics try to

---

[60] Tertullian, *Prescription against Heretics*, Ch. 21, in Alexander Roberts and James Donaldson, eds. *Ante Nicene Fathers*, 10 v. (Edinburgh: T& T Clark, reprint1997), 3: 252, 253.
[61] St. Basil of Caesarea (c.329-379), see Douglas, 110.

discount. He adds that Tradition is a guide to understanding and observing the sacraments and admits that time will not be sufficient if he attempts to recount the unwritten mysteries of the Church.[62]

St. Basil in his Treatise *On The Holy Spirit* illustrates many traditions which were well known and practiced throughout the Churches worldwide. He writes:

> Of the beliefs and practices whether generally accepted or publicly enjoyed which are preserved in the Church some we possess derived from written teaching; others we have received delivered to us "in a mystery" by the tradition of the apostles; and both of these in relations to true religion have the same force. And these no one will gainsay; -no one, at all events, who is even moderately versed in the institutions of the Church. For were we to attempt to reject such customs as having no written authority, on the ground that the importance they possess is small, we should unintentionally injure the Gospel in its very vitals; or, rather, should make our public definition a mere phrase and nothing more. For instance, to take the first and most general example, who is there who has taught us in writing to sign of the cross those who have trusted in the name of our Lord Jesus Christ? What writing has taught us to turn to the East at the prayer? Which of the saints has left us in writing the words of time invocation at the displaying of the bread of the Eucharist and the cup of blessing? For we are not, as is well known, content with what the apostle or the Gospel has recorded, but both in preface and conclusion we add other words as

---

[62] Malaty, 32.

being of great importance to the validity of the ministry, and these we derive from unwritten teaching. Moreover we bless the water of baptism and the oil of the chrism, and besides this the catechumen who is being baptized. On what written authority do we do this? Is not our authority silent and mystical tradition? Nay, by what written word is the anointing of oil itself taught? And whence comes the custom of baptizing thrice? And as to the other customs of baptism from what Scripture do we derive the renunciation of Satan and his angels? Does not this come from that unpublished and secret teaching which our fathers guarded in a silence out of the reach of curious meddling and inquisitive investigation? Well had they learnt the lesson that the awful dignity of the mysteries is best preserved by silence? What the uninitiated are not even allowed: to look at was hardly likely to be publicly paraded about in written documents. What was the meaning of the mighty Moses in not making all the parts of the tabernacle open to everyone?[63]

Here St. Basil puts emphasis on a very important rule. He asserts that there are no teachings of small importance and others of great importance. This rule should apply to both Scripture and Tradition. For example we cannot attribute less honour to some parts of Scripture because they hold organizational functions (such as I Tim. 2). In other words, he is in agreement with Debis that all Tradition and traditions are needed for salvation.

---

[63] St. Basil, *On The Holy Spirit*, Ch. XXVII, Art 66, in Philip Schaff and Henry Wace, eds. *Nicene and Post - Nicene Fathers, Second Series*, 14 v., (Edinburgh: T & T Clark, reprint 1994) 8: 40,41.

Oberman claimed that Basil in his treatise *On the Holy Spirit* initiated the idea that Christians owe equal respect and obedience to written and unwritten ecclesiastical traditions, whether they were mentioned in canonized writings or in the oral tradition handed down by the apostles through succession.[64] But Florovsky disagrees with this opinion, writing:

> At First glance one may get the impression that St. Basil introduces here a double authority and double standard-Scripture and Tradition. In Fact he was very far from doing so. His use of terms is peculiar. *Kerygmata* were for him what in the later idiom was usually denoted as "dogmas" or "doctrine" – a formal and authoritative teaching and ruling in the matters of faith,- the open or public teaching. On the Other hand, *dogmata* were for him the total complex of "unwritten habits", or, in fact, the whole structure of liturgical and sacramental life. It must be kept in mind that the concept, and the term itself "dogma," was not yet fixed by that time, -it was not yet a term with a strict and exact connotation. In any case, one should not be embarrassed by the contention of St. Basil that *dogmata* were delivered or handed down, by the Apostles. It will be a flagrant mistranslation if we render it as "in secret" The only accurate rendering is: "by the way of mysteries" that is-under the form of rites and (liturgical) usages or "Habit". In fact, it is precisely what St. Basil says himself: Most of the mysteries are communicated to us by an unwritten way.[65]

Florovsky here is defending St. Basil and re-affirming the one

---

[64] Oberman, *The Dawn of the Reformation*, 277.
[65] Florovsky, *Bible, Church, Tradition: An Eastern Orthodox View*, 86.

source of revelation theory that is Tradition. I can see St. Basil holding the whole Church life within Tradition, whether it is Scripture, believers' personal practice or public liturgical acts. He did not rank the different aspects of Tradition, but we can sense from his words that all doctrines have equal value and nothing could be missed or altered. For him such doctrines are apostolic and preserved through the daily liturgical practice of the Church without need for biblical warrant.

Bruce and Hanson find that Basil might, at first glance, look like he is attempting to turn Christianity into a mystery-religion or ecclesiastical freemasonry and to canonize a tradition of custom that earlier Christian ages had regarded as wholly secondary. Hanson comments that Basil does not "give a status as *de fide* to all existing customs or rite in use in the Eastern Orthodox Churches of his time, especially in his own diocese."[66] However, St. Basil does seem to give *de fide status* to some customs such as signing with the cross and triple immersion and he would thereby have run into difficulties with the Reformers. For St. Basil it is one source of revelation (Tradition) and each single article in it has the same authority and there is nothing that would have less importance provided that all have apostolic origins.

---

[66] Hanson R., *Tradition in the Early Church*, cited in Bruce, 127.

Tradition according to Gregory Nazianzen

St. Gregory Nazianzen (329-389) in his oration *On the Holy Spirit* explains how humanity was gradually developing in its relationship with God. He notes the move from idol-worshipping to the Law and then from the Law to the Gospel as two major earthquakes in the gradual maturity of the relationship.[67] Moreover, he avers that the apostles themselves accepted these gradual changes. He gives Paul as a model:

> Paul is a proof of this; for having at one time administered circumcision, and submitted to legal purification, he advanced till he could say, and I brethren, if I yet preach circumcision, why do I yet suffer persecution? (Gal. 5:11) His former conduct belonged to the temporary dispensation, his later to maturity.[68]

St. Gregory adds that the perfection of theology "is reached by additions."[69] He gives the example of the Lord and how he gradually proclaimed the truth to his disciples.[70] He adds:

> You see lights breaking upon us, gradually; and the order of Theology, which it is better for us to keep, neither proclaiming things too suddenly, nor yet keeping them hidden to the end. For the former course would be unscientific, the latter atheistic; and the former would be calculated to

---

[67] Gregory Nazianzen, *'On the Holy Sprit'* available online <http://www.ccel.org/fathers2/NPNF2-07/Npnf2-07-46.htm#P4606_1453815> [3rd December, 2004] Article XXV
[68] Ibid.
[69] Ibid, article XXVI
[70] Ibid

startle outsiders, the latter to alienate our own people. I will add another point to what I have said; one which may readily have come into the mind of some others, but which I think a fruit of my own thought. Our Savior had some things which, He said, could not be borne at that time by His disciples (though they were filled with many teachings), perhaps for the reasons I have mentioned; and therefore they were hidden. And again He said that all things should be taught us by the Spirit when He should come to dwell amongst us. Of these things one, I take it, was the Deity of the Spirit Himself, made clear later on when such knowledge should be seasonable and capable of being received after our Savior's restoration, when it would no longer be received with incredulity because of its marvelous character. For what greater thing than this did either He promise, or the Spirit teach. If indeed anything is to be considered great and worthy of the Majesty of God, which was either promised or taught. [71]

This is how St. Gregory shows his acceptance and the affirmation of the development in theology and revelation. However, the development of revelation mentioned by him is only part of the economy of God. What has been revealed came in a certain sequence to be gradually grasped and understood by man. Such development ended when Scripture was fully written and nothing had to be added to the revelation.

The words of St. Gregory in the previous quote could be understood not only to limit its scope to Scripture but also to

---

[71] Ibid, Article XXVII

include extra-biblical teachings. However, the Orthodox mind limits the meaning of this excerpt exclusively to Scripture, confirming the full-stature or maturity of the Church once the writing of Scripture was completed. Additionally, from an Orthodox point of view, this does not mean an acceptance or allowance of any innovations, but it rather allows for re-synthesis in the face of new challenges. Meyendorff states:

> The Divine Truth which abides in her (Church) must, therefore, always face new challenges and be expressed in new ways. The Christian message is not only to be kept unchangeable, but it must also be *understood* by those to whom it is sent by God; it must answer new questions posed by new generations. Thus enters another function of Holy Tradition: to make scripture available and understandable to a changing and imperfect world. In this world, treating problems in isolation from Tradition by simplistic references to Scripture may lead to error and heresy.[72]

Meyendorff explains the necessity of "doctrinal development" but not as an addition or continuation of revelation. He gives the example of St. Athanasius who succeeded in adding the word *homoousios* during the Council of Nicea (325) which was not scriptural but contained the scriptural truth and in a language comprehensible in his contemporary time[73]. He adds the example of calling Virgin Mary "Mother of God" "*Theotokos*" in refuting

---

[72] John Meyendorff, *Living Tradition*, (Crestwood, NY :St. Vladimir's Seminary Press, 1978), 17.
[73] Ibid, 17.

the Nestorians in council of Ephesus (431),[74] Meyendorff confirms:

> These examples were brought forth here not for the sake of polemics on the issues which they involve, but in order to illustrate the Orthodox approach to the problem of "doctrinal development", whose meaning consists neither in a sort of continuous revelation, nor in making additions to Scripture, but in solving concrete problems related to the one eternal Truth, the latter remaining essentially the same before and after the definitions.[75]

Tradition according to St. Vincent of Lérins[76]

Fr. Florovsky, in introducing Tradition according to St. Vincent starts his essay by quoting the *dictum Augustini* where Augustine says "Indeed, I should not have believed the Gospel, if the authority of the Catholic Church had not moved me."[77] He further adds the famous quote of St. Vincent: "We must hold what has been believed everywhere, always, and by all,"[78] and he asserts that these two dimensions (antiquity and the permanent consensus of the whole church) could never be separated from each other. He states that St. Vincent suggested that the true faith could be recognized by Scripture and Tradition. First, it is the authority of the Holy Scripture and then by the Tradition of the Catholic Church. At the same time, he insists that they are not two different

---

[74] Ibid, 18.
[75] Ibid, 19.
[76] St. Vincent of Lérins (d. before 450), see Douglas, 1019-1020.
[77] Florovsky, *Bible, Church, Tradition: An Eastern Orthodox View*, 73.
[78] Ibid, 73.

sources of Christian doctrine, and the Scripture was perfect and self-sufficient. His reason for using another authority was the problem of different interpretations of Scripture by individuals. This principal is in agreement with the phrase of St. Hilary of Poitiers "For Scripture is not in reading, but in the understanding". This is echoed loudly by St. Jerome as well.[79] Florovsky summarizes the relation between the two as follows:

> Tradition was not, according to St. Vincent, an independent instance, nor was it a complementary source of faith. "Ecclesiastical understanding" could not add anything to the Scripture. But it was the only means to ascertain and to disclose the true meaning of Scripture. Tradition was, in fact, the authentic interpretation of Scripture. And in this sense it was co-extensive with Scripture. Tradition was actually "Scripture rightly understood" and Scripture was for St. Vincent the only, primary and ultimate canon of Christian truth.[80]

Oberman selected five essential requirements from St. Vincent to validate canonizing the Tradition of the Fathers. First, he insisted that not one or two Fathers but all the Fathers must hold it. Moreover, the consensus has to be exactly the same. Thirdly, their opinion should be openly and explicitly formulated. Furthermore, it should be repeatedly advanced; and finally, it should be continuously held, written and taught. Here he asserts the same principal of the concept of one authoritative exegetical tradition

---
[79] Ibid, 74, 75.
[80] Ibid.

against the two sources of revelation.[81]

Father John Whiteford expounds this idea as he sees a need for Tradition to be believed always and without any interruption. He asserts that Tradition neither grows nor changes, but is always kept in the Church since if the Church ceased to have the truth, 'even for a single day,' then the gates of hell would prevail against it. This would be absurd, for God's unfailing promise is "And I also say to you that you are Peter, and on this rock I will build my church, and the gates of Hades shall not prevail against it" (Matthew 16:18).[82] He adds, if there was any doubt about the Church's faithfulness in preserving the apostolic Tradition, then there would be doubt in her fidelity in preserving the Scripture.[83]

Florovsky describes Vincent in terms of Oberman's Tradition I. He sees Tradition as a tool for Scriptural interpretations and not as some extra-biblical teachings. Oberman sees Vincent in terms of Tradition II, and he observes that the five conditions necessary to canonize the teaching as Tradition are allowing for extra-biblical teachings. However, from an Orthodox view, the conditions of Vincent are valid and acceptable for extra-biblical teachings. Additionally, these conditions give weight to the

---

[81] Oberman, *The Dawn of the Reformation*, 280.
[82] John Whiteford, *Sola Scripture, In The Vanity Of Their Minds*. Available [Internet] <http://orthodoxinfo.com/inquirers/tca_solascriptura.htm> [25th November 2003].
[83] Ibid.

consistency between Tradition and Scripture without any room for contradictions.

Schaff sees that there is not even a *consensus patrum* in some matters of faith as in the doctrine of free will, predestination, or the atonement. A certain freedom of divergent private opinions is the indispensable condition of all progress of thought, and precedes the ecclesiastical settlement of every article of faith. He adds:

> Vincentius is thoroughly Catholic in the spirit and tendency of his work, and has not the most remote conception of the free Protestant study of the Scriptures. But on the other hand he would have as little toleration for new dogmas. He wished to make tradition not an independent source of knowledge and rule of faith by the side of the Holy Scriptures, but only to have it acknowledged as the true interpreter of Scripture, and as a bar to heretical abuse. The criterion of the antiquity of a doctrine, which he required, involves apostolicity, hence agreement with the spirit and substance of the New Testament. The church, says he, as the solicitous guardian of that which is in trusted to her, changes, diminishes, increases nothing. Her sole effort is to shape, or confirm, or preserve the old. Innovation is the business of heretics not of orthodox believers. The canon of Scripture is complete in itself, and more than sufficient. But since all heretics appeal to it, the authority of the church must be called in as the rule of interpretation, and in this we must follow universality, antiquity, and consent. It is the custom of the Catholics, says he in the same work, to prove the true faith in two ways: first by the authority of the holy Scriptures, then by the tradition of the Catholic church; not because the

canon alone is not of itself sufficient for all things, but on account of the many conflicting interpretations and perversions of the Scriptures. In the same spirit says pope Leo I.: "It is not permitted to depart even in one word from the doctrine of the Evangelists and the Apostles, nor to think otherwise concerning the Holy Scriptures, than the blessed apostles and our fathers learned and taught."[84]

Schaff's claim that there is not even a *consensus patrum* in some matters of faith is true in a way. However, some of these doctrines are taught by some Fathers in some places for a certain period only. For example, St. Epiphanius of Salamis believed that icons were illegitimate and yet, later, the second council of Nicaea decreed that they were legitimate.[85] Nevertheless, the teachings of St. Epiphanies lacked the consensus of the Fathers and the universality of this doctrine at that time, so it was finally overturned by the Church Fathers in universal consensus at the second council of Nicaea.

In some other articles of faith such as free will and predestination there is always an ecclesial universal consensus, however, this does not stop individuals from thinking and presenting different views as well. For example, in the doctrine of the free will, the consensus is "[i]n our fallen state the human will is sick but not dead; and, although more difficult, it is still possible

---

[84] Schaff, 3: 472.
[85] *Icons of Macedonia: Beginnings- The Iconoclasts versus the Cult of Icons.* Available [Internet] < http://www.soros.org.mk/konkurs/019/eng/txt01.htm> [14th March 2004].

for humans to choose the good."[86] This teaching is fulfilling the criteria stated by St. Vincent. St. Cyril of Jerusalem (315-386) says "[t]he soul is self-governed: and though the devil can suggest, he has not the power to compel against the will."[87] This doctrine is stated in the *Confessions of Faith* of Dositheos the Patriarch of Jerusalem (1641-1701) and affirmed by the council of Jerusalem in 1672. Meanwhile, this did not prevent Augustine (354-430) from saying "free will is destroyed."[88] In the Orthodox Church, this means that the councils declare the doctrines which are necessary for the public without preventing the theologians from presenting their views.

Conclusion

For the Orthodox, Tradition is a wider word and Scripture is an element of it, thus there is a complete harmony between Scripture, Tradition and Church. So, no part of this process can be given priority over another (e.g. Scripture over the Fathers, etc.) because they are believed to form a harmonious whole. Scouteris describes the relation between Church, Scripture and Tradition as follows:

---

[86] Kallistos Ware, *How Are We Saved? The understanding of Salvation in the Orthodox Tradition*, (Minneapolis, Minnesota: Light and Life publishing, 1996), 33.
[87] Cyril of Jerusalem, *Catechetical Lectures, 4: 21*. Available [Internet] <http://www.ccel.org/fathers2/NPNF2-07/Npnf2-07-09.htm#P452_92480> >[14th March].
[88] Augustine, *The Enchiridion*, 30. Available [Internet] <http://www.iclnet.org/pub/resources/text/ipb-e/epl-01/agenc-02.txt> [14th March 2004].

Those who separate Holy Scripture, Tradition and Church come to the false conclusion that either Scripture is superior to the Church and Tradition, or that the Church is Superior to Scripture. The first opinion is to be found among Protestant theologians, the later in Roman Catholic theology. This hyperbole leads to an alteration of the meaning of the Church, either to an under-evaluation (subordination) or to an over-evaluation. By placing the Bible over and above the Church and Tradition we destroy the balance, we corrupt its canonical position, and take the first step towards an individualistic theology outside the Church. On the other hand, the idea that the Church is superior to Holy Scripture leads to the opinion that the Church is able to elicit every dogma from within herself. Only if we accept that the Church, Tradition and Scripture are neither separated nor confused, being united without confusion, will we be able to understand that the Church alone is she who can find the true meaning of Holt Scripture, just as the Son alone is he who is able to understand the words of the Father.[89]

Orthodox theologians consider that any schism in Church history is a result of a deviation from the One Holy Tradition. In light of this understanding, Konstantinidis confirms that the Great Schism between West and East in the eleventh century was a disagreement with the One Holy Tradition.[90] Additionally, Ware asserts that the primary cause for the break-up of Western Christendom in the sixteenth century was the separation between theology and

---

[89] Scouteris, 37.
[90] Chrysostomos Konstantinidis, *The Significance Of The Eastern And Western Traditions Within Christendom*, in *The Orthodox Church In Ecumenical Movement*, (Geneva: World Council of Churches, 1978), 225.

mysticism, between liturgy and personal devotion which was the case at the Late Middle Ages. Whilst he asserts that Orthodoxy always works to avoid such divisions,[91] he adds:

> All True Orthodox theology is mystical; just as mysticism divorced from theology becomes subjective and heretical, so, theology when it is not mystical, degenerates into an arid scholasticism, 'academic' in the bad sense of the word. Theology, mysticism, spirituality, moral rules, worship, art; these things must not be kept in a separate compartment. Doctrine cannot be understood unless it is prayed; a theologian, said Evagrius, is one who knows how to pray, and he who prays in spirit and in truth is by that very act a theologian. And doctrine, if it is to be prayed, must also be lived; theology without action, as Saint Maximus put it, is the theology of demons.[92]

The Orthodox Patristic Tradition has no contradictions with the Scripture, thus it was accepted in the East and the West before the Great Schism without clear problems except for the Iconoclastic Controversy. Iconoclasm has been sorted out in the second council of Nicaea (787). Consequently, local customs such as clerical vestments and kissing hands of the clergy have never been canonized in the Orthodox Church as essential doctrines for salvation. There is some disagreement among Orthodox theologians as to whether there is a difference between Tradition and customs (or 'traditions') and as to whether all such customs are binding to Orthodox Christians.

---

[91] Ware, *The Orthodox Church*, 215.
[92] Ware, *The Orthodox Church*, 215.

However, the Orthodox Church needs to draw a clear line between Tradition and Customs. Such identification will help to show what is needed for salvation and what could be accepted as local customs, which understandably vary from place to place and community to community. In contemporary practices, according to the Orthodox Church—the Holy Synod is the highest authority and is able to distinguish and judge any doctrines or teaching. The Holy Synod is not infallible and in case of any misjudging, it would be rectified by the Synod in other sessions. To posit an example that will clarify this point, Cyril Lucaris (1572-1638) the patriarch of Constantinople who tried to bring the Orthodox closer to a Calvinistic theological position was condemned in 1672 by the great Orthodox Synod of Jerusalem.[93]

The Fathers are highly regarded in the Orthodox Patristic Tradition, without making them infallible. Werckmeister confirms the perpetual fatherhood of the Fathers, just as the first four ecumenical councils: Nicaea, Ephesus, Constantinople and Chalcedon were of equated with the four gospels throughout the Middle Ages.[94] Florovsky follows the same line and sees that the usual introduction of the ecumenical councils is "following the Holy Fathers". He adds that the decision regarding the Holy Icons in the Seven Ecumenical council also opens in this way: "Following the divinely inspired teaching of the Holy Fathers and the Tradition

---

[93] Douglas, 607.
[94] Jean Werckmeister, *The Reception of The Church Fathers In Canon Law*, in Irena Backus, eds. *The Reception of the Church Fathers in the West, From Carolingians to The Maurists*, 2 v., (Leiden: E.J. Brill, 1997), 1:56.

of the Catholic Church..."[95]

The Orthodox Patristic understanding of Tradition would have helped the forerunners of the Reformation and the Reformers to accept the true part of Tradition, which was the one true Tradition before the Great Schism. However, the unclear distinction between Tradition and customs would have complicated the matter but not to the level it is today.

---

[95] Florovsky, *Bible, Church, Tradition: An Eastern Orthodox View*, 105.

3 THE SOURCES OF REVELATION IN THE MEDIEVAL PERIOD

The purpose of this Chapter is to map the gradual rise of the tension between Scripture and Tradition, and to investigate how far the Latin Church of that time deviated from the Orthodox Patristic understanding of Tradition. It will outline some of the innovated doctrines that started to appear in the West after the great schism. This chapter covers the age from the late medieval times until the period of the forerunners of the Reformation.

The tension started to appear in the West after the Great Schism (1054). Before the Great Schism the Church lived with Tradition I and Tradition II[96] without any serious conflicts. The church accepted extra-biblical teachings as part of its truth in as far as there were no contradictions with Scripture. An additional condition[97] for canonizing any extra-biblical teaching was avoidance of any innovations.

This chapter will deal with the historical relation between Scripture and Tradition during the twelfth century and the early part of the thirteenth century, which is considered to be the most

---

[96] Defined later in this chapter.
[97] As explained in Chapter 1.

significant period of ideological divergence between these two terms by Oberman. This period started with a powerful papacy and ended with a confused, and weak, papacy. This Chapter will depend mainly on George Tavard[98] and Oberman[99] for the analysis of this period of critical development. The study will introduce some theologians of this period who debated the changes that occurred. In particular, it will study carefully the rise of the tension between conciliarists and canon lawyers in the fourteenth century.

In looking at the fourteenth century I intend to present an extensive study of contemporary theologians such as Occam, Gerson, d'Ailly, Biel and Wessel of Gansfort. In addition to this, one of the most important documents in the late medieval period (written by John Brevicoxa) is examined in detail. Brevicoxa was the first to explain the differences, meanings and the rules for accepting Tradition I and Tradition II. The study will show how the nominalists Occam, Gerson and d'Ailly stand for Tradition II against, Wycliffe, Huss, and Gansfort who stood for Tradition I and against Tradition II.

An examination of the heresies of the Late Medieval times

---

[98] Catholic Priest was Professor of theology at the Methodist Theological School in Ohio, from which he retired in 1990 as a Professor Emeritus. For more see: *George Tavard Biography*, available on line <http://www.assumption.edu/brighton/tavard/english/biography.htm>[May 5th 2004].

[99] Oberman (1930-2001) Reformed Church minister and Professor at Harvard University since 1966. For more see: *In Memoriam : Heiko Augsutinus Oberman (1930-2001)*. Available [Internet] <http://info-center.ccit.arizona.edu/~dlmrs/DH09,2.html> [5th May 2004].

is undertaken. It summarizes the rise of the Waldensians who were considered the first to rebel against the Catholic tradition of that time. This is followed by considering the rise of public tensions, which accompanied the rise of heresies such as the Wycliffites and the Hussites. Both Huss and Wycliffe have been considered by many historians as the forerunners for the Reformation. Finally, at the end of the chapter a conclusion is furnished which summarizes the circumstances which paved the way to the Reformation.

Heiko Oberman on "Tradition I" and "Tradition II"

For the outset of the chapter, I would like to define what is meant by Tradition I and Tradition II. For demonstration see figure (1) page 35 then compare it with figure (2) page 36 to note the difference between the Orthodox Church and the West.

According to Oberman, the single-source or exegetical tradition of Scripture which holds within itself its interpretation is called "Tradition I". Tradition I should be seen as a reaction against the increasing recognition of the Basilean two source theory[100] which shall be explained later in this chapter. He explains Tradition I:

> Tradition I, then, represents the sufficiency of Holy Scripture as understood by the Fathers and doctors of the Church. In the case of disagreement between these interpreters, Holy Scripture has the final authority. The horizontal concept of Tradition is by no means denied here,

---

[100]Heiko Oberman, *The Harvest of Medieval Theology, Gabriel Biel and Late Medieval Nominalism* (Cambridge, Massachusetts: Harvard University Press 1963), 371.

but rather understood as the mode of reception of the *fides* or *veritas* contained in Holy Scripture. Since the appeal to extra-scriptural tradition is rejected, the validity of ecclesiastical traditions and *consuetudines* is not regarded as "self-supporting" but depends on its relation to the faith handed down by God in Holy Scripture.[101]

In other words, Tradition is derived from Scripture, which, in turn, is derived from God. The holders of Tradition I insist that unless a doctrine or practice was explicitly mentioned in Scripture, no one should be obliged to follow it. However Reformation radicals like Andreas Bodenstein Carlstadt believed that Christians should not do anything that is not explicitly commanded in Scripture. For example, because the Scripture does not command the believer to make the sign of the cross, then they should not do it.[102] Tradition I is acceptable so far as it represented the Church's cumulative attempt across history to interpret the Scripture, but it would always have to derive its authority from Scripture and from no other source.

According to Oberman the two-source theory, which allows for extra-biblical oral traditions, is called "Tradition II." Exceptional importance has been vested in John 20:23 "Now Jesus did many other signs in the presence of the disciples which are not written in this book." These extra scriptural teachings used the Basilean passage quoted in Chapter I as a base and an authentic

---

[101] Ibid, 372.
[102] Schaff, 7:457.

theological argument. This put only two options in front of the theologians of that time, either to call for doctrinal reformation or to discard the claim to a biblical warrant for doctrine. He adds:

> The second concept of tradition, Tradition II, refers to the written and unwritten part of the apostolic message as approved by the Church. Here it is not the function of the doctors of Holy Scripture but that of the bishops which is relatively more stressed. The hierarchy is seen to have its "own" oral tradition, to a certain undefined extent independent, not of the Apostles, but of what is recorded in the canonical books. Ecclesiastical traditions, including canon law, are invested with the same degree of authority as that of Holy Scripture.[103]

Tradition I

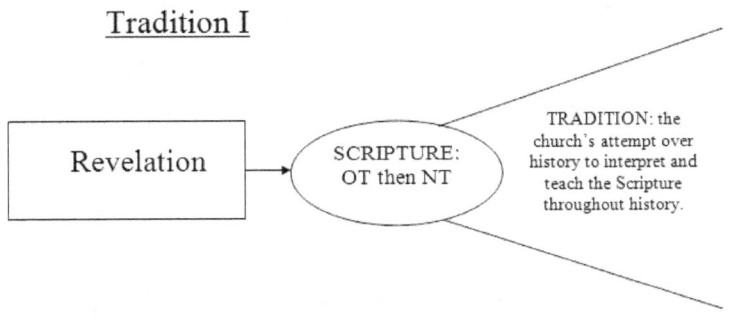

---

[103] Oberman, *The Harvest of Medieval Theology*, 373.

Tradition II

```
┌──────────────┐      ┌─────────────┐
│              │ ───→ │  SCRIPTURE  │ ─────→
│  Revelation  │      └─────────────┘
│              │      ┌─────────────┐
└──────────────┘ ───→ │  UNWRITTEN  │ ─────→
                      │  TRADITION  │
                      └─────────────┘
```

Figure (1)

A clear distinction of responsibility in relation to the two traditions is seen in one of Ambrosius of Speier's[104] sermons, which was published on the eve of the Reformation. He asserts that the interpretation of the Scripture is the theologian's duty, while the decisions of legal cases are the Pope's task[105]. He adds in a *sardonic* manner:

> You may rely on the doctors of Scripture in all matters regarding the interpretation of Scripture... unless it regards the sacraments and the articles of faith; since the power to interpret a dubious law has been granted not to the theologians but to the Pope.[106]

Tradition I, according to Oberman, is accepted by the Orthodox

---

[104] Carmelite preacher.
[105] Oberman, *The Harvest of Medieval Theology*, 373.
[106] Ambrosius of Speier, *Liber sermonum quadragesimalium de floribus sapientiae*, (Basel, 1516; sermon 37, fol.265 F, quoted in Oberman, *The Harvest of Medieval Theology*, 373.

Church as the cumulative interpretations of the Scriptures by the approved Church Fathers. Tradition II was accepted in the East and the West before the Great Schism as both were keeping to the One Holy Orthodox Tradition. After the great Schism the West innovated a lot of doctrines as discussed later in this chapter.

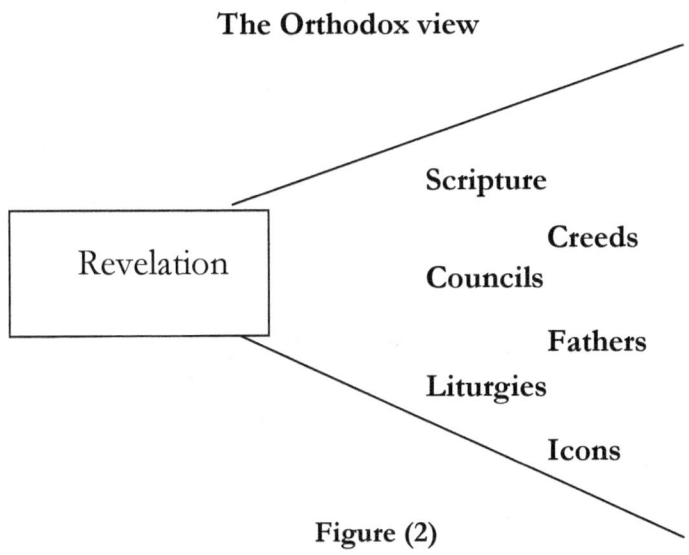

Figure (2)

Developments in Late Medieval Theology

Although Patristic theology came to an end at the turn of the seventh century, there is no doubt a continuous link between Patristic theology and the medieval schools throughout the empire of Charlemagne.[107] Tavard confirms that although the greater part of the Fathers' writings were not readily available, the Spirit with

---

[107] Tavard, *Holy Writ or Holy Church, The Crises of the Protestant Reformation*, 12.

which they tried to provide an understanding of the faith survived in the writers of the Middle Ages.[108]

Tavard sees the twelfth and the thirteenth centuries as faithful to the Patristic conception of "Scripture alone." He gives many examples of how the writers of these centuries have used and understood the word Tradition. He cites Peter Cantor using the term *traditiones* to refer to the monastic life or the liturgical customs, and Andrew of St. Victor opposing the exegetical *traditiones* of Jews to those of Christians.[109] This demonstrates that the word Tradition at this period had a wide meaning that could include the extra-biblical teachings. However, it also shows a Church recognition of the difference between the Living Christian Tradition and the Jewish non-saving traditions and customs.

Tavard comments on how some medieval theologians' of the twelfth and thirteenth centuries (such as Rupert of Deutz) understood the authority of Scripture:

> On account of his intelligence and learning, (according to Rupert) Paul goes with Cyprian and Augustine. This quaint idea raises a question on the Scriptural canon. The suggestion seems to be that Paul differs somehow from the other Apostles though his writings are part of Scriptures as such. Rupert of Deuz attributes a special place to Paul: "Let us investigate all the extension of Holy Scripture, from the beginning of Genesis to the summit of the Gospel and to that corner

---
[108] Ibid, 12.
[109] Ibid, 20.

where Paul, the junior among the Apostles, stands with his letters". Whatever may be implied here, medieval writers commonly saw a sharp distinction between the power of Christ manifesting himself through Scripture and the inadequacy of the inspired authors, Abelard pushed this to a Paradox: "What cause is there for surprise if in the Gospel also some elements have been wrapped by the writers' ignorance?" The power of Christ breaks through in spite of that. The medieval mind was not fundamentalist.[110]

The nature of the conflict in the thought of the Middle Ages, as seen by Oberman, was not simply between Scripture and Tradition; rather there were two debatable points. The first point is that Holy Scripture has canonical authority (there being no conflict with Tradition) only within the church through the interpretation of gifted doctors. He describes it in a nutshell: "The history of obedient interpretation is the Tradition of the Church." The second point is that Tradition has a wider sense. The argument is that not everything necessary was written by the Apostles, in particular what Christ taught them in the forty days after his resurrection. Such teachings, which are not found in Scripture, were taught by the Apostles and practiced in the Church and handed down from generation to generation. This he sums up saying[111]:

> In the first case, Tradition was seen as the instrumental vehicle of Scripture which brings the

---

[110] Ibid, 13-14.
[111] Oberman, *The Forerunners of the Reformation*, 54.

contents of Holy Scripture to life in a constant dialogue between doctors, Scripture and the Church; in the second case Tradition was seen as the authoritative vehicle of divine truth, embedded in Scripture but overflowing in extra-scriptural apostolic tradition handed down through episcopal succession.[112]

The second case of Tradition described by Oberman is much closer to the Orthodox position outlined in Chapter I. However, the overflowing of the extra-scriptural apostolic Tradition is seen as unchangeable and not subject to any innovations at any later times. The outer form of Tradition may vary according to the local cultures and customs provided this does not produce contradictions with Scriptures.

Whilst Oberman confirms that, in both East and West, early Patristic literature agrees on the sufficiency of Holy Scripture and that any denial of this was a mark of heresy, he adds that later St. Basil in the East in his treatise *On the Holy Spirit* first stated that the Christians owed equal respect and obedience to written and unwritten ecclesiastical traditions, whether contained in the canonical writings or in the secret oral tradition handed down through Apostolic succession.[113] Half a century later, St. Augustine introduced the idea to the West. Oberman comments on this development:

> While repeatedly asserting the primacy of the

---
[112] Ibid, 55.
[113] Ibid, 55.

> Scripture, Augustine himself does not contrast this at all with the authority of the Catholic Church "... I would not believe the Gospel, unless the authority of the Catholic Church moved me (*commovit me*)" Here the Church must be understood to have an authority to direct (*commovere*) the believer to the door which leads to the fullness of the Word itself [...] the moving authority of the Church becomes in the late medieval versions the Church's approval or creation of Holy Scripture.... Indeed the voice of the fourteenth century Augustinian, Gregory of Rimini (1358), protesting that Augustine meant merely a practical priority of the Church over Scripture, went largely unheard.[114]

According to the definition of Tradition in Chapter I, neither St. Basil nor St. Augustine promoted priority of Church or Scripture. Such a clash never existed in their times. Nevertheless, the Church is assumed to be historically prior to Scripture although Scriptural teaching was in the Church from the very first day, yet it was not written and canonized. Scripture was lived and practiced in the church -within the one Holy Tradition- before it was written. There was not a call for equal respect for written and unwritten ecclesial traditions. Tradition as a whole was to be respected and obeyed. It includes Scripture, Liturgies and other things as explained in detail in the previous chapter.

Just before the end of the thirteenth century Henry of

---

[114] Ibid, 56.

Ghent[115] wrote a prologue that indicated a change of outlook regarding Scripture. This prologue contained twenty articles including 117 questions, one of which deals with the authority of sacred Scripture. He asks "Must we rather believe the authorities of this doctrine (i.e. Sacred Scripture) than those of the church, or the other way a round"(Art.10,O.I). In addition, Henry suggests that such discrepancy may occur between the Church of God as an organization and the Church as a community of the believers considered as the Church. Tavard sees this distinction as an important aspect of Reformers thinking when they thought that the community, which was then called the Church, was condemned by Scripture, which gives a peculiar significance to the solution of Henry.[116]

Henry sees that in the case that the majority of the believers dissent and renounce the faith, by mistake or malice, the Church will still survive with a handful of just men:

> In the impossible situation where a Christian would see all other Christians leave the faith, Scripture would provide the rock on which that man could stand alone, over against the judgments of the others, over against "What seems to be the Church". Thus, indeed a believer, knowing Sacred Scripture and having found Christ in it, believes the words of Christ in it rather than any preacher, rather even than the testimony of the Church,

---

[115](d. 1293) Theologian and philosopher. Born at Ghent, he became archdeacon successively of Bruges and Tournai and taught in Paris where he became the most outstanding secular master for many years, for more see Douglas, 462.
[116] Tavard, 23.

> since he believes in the Church already on account of Scripture. And supposing that the Church herself taught contrary to Scripture, he would not believe her" (n. 10)[117]

Later, at the beginning of the fourteenth century, Gerald of Bologna's [118] prologue in his commentary on the Sentences opened fire on the alleged opposition between 'Holy Writ' and 'Holy Church,' where he based his arguments on Henry's twenty articles. Yet he was free enough to criticize Henry in his twelve articles constituting his treatment.[119] He put this clearly:

> The authority of Scripture and that of the Catholic Church under the guidance and ruling of the Holy Spirit are one and the same. And thus one must uniformly believe in it as such.[120]

Gerald argues with Henry's ideas and rejects them one by one and finally asks: "Should neophytes trust the Church rather than the Scripture, while the adult in faith would trust Scripture rather than what seems to be the Church?" Then he comments that this way of speaking does not seem truly reasonable.[121] Tavard confirms that although Gerald stressed the absolute coherence of Scripture and the Church, he ends with the following note, which does not ultimately differ from that of Henry:

> If, however, the Church is meant for the men

---

[117] Henry of Ghent, *Commentary on the Sentences*, quoted in Tavard, 25.
[118] Gerald of Bologna (d.1317) a Carmelite and author of an unpublished *Summa*.
[119] Tavard, 25.
[120] Gerald, *Commentary on the Sentences*, cited in Tavard, 25-26.
[121] Tavard 25.

themselves considered in their own nature, then one must rather believe in Scripture than in men. Scripture stems from the authority of God. And much more so if 'Church' means men who have strayed from faith. Supposing that all, with only one exception, had strayed from faith and Holy Scripture, one should believe this one rather than the others, even though he would not constitute the Church, since the Church is, properly speaking, an assembly of believers and he would be alone. When Church is taken in these senses, one must believe Scripture rather than the Church.(p.359)[122]

Tavard's comment on Henry's solution above was not relevant before the Great Schism as the Scripture and the Church were not in contradiction. This is confirmed by Henry when he notes the condition that Scripture and Church are both under the guidance and the ruling of the Holy Spirit. This means that the Church will never be only one person as he said. The Holy Spirit is always leading her and The Tradition is the guard for this harmony between Church and Scripture.

William of Occam[123] opposed John XXII and Benedict XII (who were contemporaries of each other), insisting that the rule of faith is the Sacred Scripture and the doctrine of the universal Church, which cannot err, and not through the Supreme

---

[122] Gerald, *Commentary on the Sentences*, quoted in Tavard, 26.
[123] William of Ockham (1300—59), an English Franciscan, was an adversary of Pope John XXII, excommunicated in 1328, his career marked the beginning of Nominalism, see: Douglas, 1049.

Pontiff (if he opposes it).[124] Tavard sees him from another point of view when he rejects all non-Scriptural teaching:

> The only truths that are to be considered Catholic and necessary to salvation are explicitly or implicitly stated in the Canon of the Bible ... All other truths, which neither are inserted in the Bible nor can be formally and necessarily inferred from its contents, are not to be held as Catholic, even if they are stated in the writings of the Fathers or the definitions of the Supreme Pontiffs, and even if they are believed by all the faithful. To assent to them firmly through faith, or for their sake to bind the human reason or intellect, is not necessary for salvation.[125]

Oberman sees Occam, Gerson, and d'Ailly as nominalistic conciliarists holding to Tradition II as an extreme significant attitude against the canon lawyers. He adds that this attitude towards the curia leads Gerson to stress, as Huss did, the opposition between the human legal traditions and the divine law. He affirms that Occam does not pit *sola scriptura* against canon law but more precisely that Occam assented to well-established legal tradition (i.e. Tradition II prior to Great Schism) against curialistic innovations.[126] Occam in his *Dialogue against Heretics* treats the question of "What truths are Catholic?" as follows:

> They think that Christians are not allowed to disagree with five sorts of truths: first with what is

---
[124] *Tractatus contra Joannem XXII*, in Richard *Scholz, Unbekannte Kirchen-politische Streitschriften*, 1904, vol.2, 398, quoted in Tavard, 31.
[125] Occam, *Dialogue against the Heretics*, BK II, CH. 3, quoted in Tavard, 31.
[126] Oberman, *The Harvest of the medieval Theology*, 378-380.

said in the Holy Scripture, or what can be inferred therefrom through necessary reasoning; second, with the truths that have come from the Apostles by the word of mouth or in the writings of the faithful, even though they may not be found in the Sacred Scriptures and may not be concluded with certainty from the Scripture alone; third, with the contents of truthful chronicles and histories; fourth, with what may be manifestly concluded from truths of the first and second kind only, or from one of them combined with a truth of the third category; fifth, with the truths which God, besides the truths revealed to the Apostles, has revealed or even inspired to others, or which he would again reveal or even inspire, once that revelation or inspiration has or would have reached, without possibility of doubt, the universal Church.[127]

Oberman comments on these five conditions for accepting the truths saying that Occam allowed for the development of doctrine. He sees his discussion on the Immaculate Conception of the Virgin Mary as evidence for that. He finds Occam rejecting the claim that a new doctrine can be revealed and concludes that the Church has to rely on one of the two sources: Scriptural and extra-scriptural revelation.[128]

Occam's conditions for the Catholic (universal) truths are wide and leave many gaps for innovations. The first and the second conditions are Orthodox, Patristic and coherent to the Orthodox Tradition. In the other hand, the fourth and the fifth conditions are

---

[127] Occam, *Dialogue against Heretics*, (op. cit. BK II, Ch. 5) quoted in Tavard, 35.
[128] Oberman, *The Harvest of the Medieval theology*, 380, 381.

very wide and became the source of all innovations after the Great Schism. The third condition should be taken carefully because not all chronicles and histories are truthful or biblical enough to be considered as Catholic truth.

D'Ailly[129] in his understanding of the relation between Scripture and Tradition insisted on the high authority of the doctors of Scripture. He sides with those who uphold Tradition II, which is subject to theological discussion. In his treatise on the relation of the Church and the Law, d'Ailly emphasizes that there is only one law, which is the law of Christ. This *'sola lex'* is against *sola scriptura*, because it can be a written document or spoken law; since before the New Testament was written, the Church already existed. He asserts that the superiority of the Church over scripture has applied since the time of Christ, and the Church stands above Holy Scripture since the biblical authors were already members of the Church before they wrote the books of the Bible.[130]

The Orthodox Church accepts that the biblical authors were members of the church before they wrote the books. However, the Orthodox Church believes that the Scriptures were taught, preached and practiced by the whole Church before they were written. So, the said Church superiority never exists. The whole message was there at all times. But it begins to be written down according to the Church's need under the guidance of the

---

[129] Pierre d'Ailly (1350-1420) is a French cardinal and theologian. Born in Compiégne, graduated from Navarre in 1363. For more see Douglas, 280.
[130] Oberman, *The Harvest of the Medieval theology*, 382, 285.

Holy Spirit. There is a co-dependency rather than a hierarchical relationship between the Church and revealed truth.

Gerson[131] is described by Philip Hughes as a great and pious religious thinker, preacher, and writer. Hughes adds that no one had anything like the prestige of this most attractive man—the Chancellor of the University of Paris in the hour when the university dominated the life of Christendom.[132] Gerson defends the sufficiency of Holy Scripture as containing all the truths necessary for salvation, but without embracing the *sola scriptura* concept but in the sense of Tradition I. He stresses in his treatise against Huss that Scripture cannot be isolated and it should be understood with the help of Tradition including the canon law. Furthermore, he gives the Church a theoretical priority over the Holy Scripture, since the Church is the judge separating the canonical books from the non-canonical books. At the same time, he believes in a second category of truths, which are received by the church through apostolic succession.[133] In his attempt to deny the non-existence of some saving doctrines in the Scripture, he claims that such truths are contained in Scripture according to one of the degrees of the Catholic truths which are defined later in this

---

[131] Jean Charlier De Gerson (1363-1429) French theologian and church leader, he succeeded his friend and teacher Pierre d'Ailly, he schooled in nominalism of William of Occam. For more see Douglas, 409-410.
[132] P. Hughes, *A History of the Church to the Eve of the Reformation*, (London: Sheed and Ward, reprint 1976) Vol. 3, 452-3.
[133] Oberman, *The Harvest of the Medieval Theology*, 385-6

chapter.[134]

In his sermon from Constance, Gerson asserts that papal authority is only a matter of expediency, a practical device to ensure good government, and that the general councils may judge the pope not only for heresy, for obstinacy in sin and also for opposition to the council. For him the Pope functions as the executive organ within the church, whilst the legislative power remains with the general council.[135] He had wanted a decree that the section of Canon of Constance about the supremacy of General Councils over the popes should be carved on the facade of every church.[136]

The Orthodox Tradition agrees with Gerson and accepts Tradition I. However, it disagrees with his expression of a second-degree category of truths. It seems here that Gerson is puzzled about a distinction between customs and Tradition. Such puzzling is a result of the non-existence of a clear line between Tradition needed for salvation and local customs. Before the Great Schism this confusion was not under discussion as Tradition was one and customs were varied and accepted as such. The case of Cyril of Lucaris (which explained in chapter one) is an example of Gerson's words that the Church could condemn the head of the church whether Bishop, Archbishop or Pope.

---

[134] Tavard, 52
[135] Hughes, Vol. 3, 275
[136] Ibid, 318

It is obvious that Gerson's attempt to downplay the supremacy of the Pope was a reaction to many of the extremists' canon lawyers. Tavard quotes some of them:

> Johannes Andreae (d. 1348), who was the master of a whole generation of canon lawyers, had commented: "the pope is wonderful, for he holds the power of God on earth: he is the vicar of him to whom the earth and the fullness of the universe belong". According to William de Amidanis, "The Pope is like God" (p.55). "As the sky, on account of its width, contains everything that under it, likewise the power of the Pope contains all power, priestly and kingly, heavenly and earthly, so that the Pope can say: all power has been given me in heaven and on earth"(p.89). The anonymous *Speculum judiciale* adds "In everything and everywhere he may do and say whatever he pleases"(p.50). He moreover enjoys a creative power in the field of moral obligations, whose nature changes according to his will: "He creates out of nothing, changing the nature of things" (p.51). In the same line Tancred marvelled : "He creates out of nothing" (p.51). And though the famous Panormitanus was himself in the conciliarists camp, he wrote: " The Pope may do whatever God may do" (p.51). "Whatever is done by the authority of the Pope is done by the authority of God"[137]

Gerson attempts to resolve the problem of authority in the church by defining six degrees of Catholic truths; all of them related to the Scriptures in different ways, Tavard summarizes them as follows:

---

[137] Tavard, 47-8.

The first degree is distinctly written black on white in the Biblical canon. The second comprises "Truths determined by the Church, which have been conveyed by the Apostles through undoubted continuous successions": let us say, apostolic traditions recognized as such by the Church. The third is made of post-apostolic revelations. These are binding on those to whom they were addressed. The Church herself may be the recipient of such revelation. We know it explicitly though prophecies and miracles, or implicitly " through the common testimony of the whole Church or of a General Council adequately representing her, this testimony being conveyed by legitimate succession from those who manifestly received such revelations to their followers. The fourth degree comprises all conclusions drawn from the first three. "Sacred canons" are placed in this category: "If we look at them carefully, those canons are no other than conclusions drawn or derived from the theological principles, that is, from the gospels and other canonical books". (*Recommendatio*, consid. x.col. 890). In the fifth degree we have conclusions that are only probable or that include a non-revealed premise. The sixth degree is reserved to pious truths "where devout piety rather than absolute truth is aimed at", provided that they do not favor superstition.[138]

Gerson's six degrees of Catholic truths raise problems similar to those ones of Occam. The first and the second degrees are Orthodox and Patristic. But the third degree, which is post-apostolic revelation, is the mother of most innovated doctrines after the Great Schism—such as the infallibility of the Pope and

---

[138] Tavard, 52-3.

the Immaculate Conception of the Virgin Mary. Fourth, fifth and sixth degrees are wide, vague and undetermined and leave a wide door to more innovations.

Amongst the significant men of this era with conciliarist-like tendencies was Nicholas de Clemanges (1360-1440), a secular priest and secretary to Pope Benedict XIII. In his time he was considered to be a theologian of the very first rank. He insisted that the church is in need of General Councils to determine her faith, but rebuked such councils for defining matters that not strictly pertain to the faith. He sees that the church and the councils have erred when they lacked the study of the divine Scripture and the writings of the Church Fathers.[139] Tavard sums up the opinion of the conciliaristic scholars:

> It is now patent that the main conciliarists are not thoroughly at one when it comes to defining the rule of faith. This would be Scripture and its meaning (Gerson), or Revelation in Scripture and outside of it, both to the Apostles and to the Later Church (d'Ailly), or Scripture and the Fathers (Clemanges). In spite of their differences, the first two include post-apostolic revelations in the rule of faith. The danger was that councils were thus in the way of becoming the official recipients of post-apostolic revelations, Clemanges was therefore wise in asking that councils should justify their doctrine by appealing to Scripture and to the Fathers.[140]

---

[139] Tavard, 55.
[140] Tavard, 56.

It is worth mentioning here that after the Great Schism, with nearly every Council, the Roman Church was adding or confirming a new innovated doctrine without either biblical or Patristic warrants. The cry for a council to determine the articles of faith and to exclude any innovations went unheard and led to the Reformation, as explained in the next chapter.

Tavard asserts that the fourteenth century witnessed the remarkable cleavage between Scripture and Church, although the Fathers and medieval Schoolmen saw the two in harmony and coherence. He adds that once the split took place in theory, the daily life of the believer in the church was affected because reading the Word of God was 'ministered and understood' by the Church.[141] Similarly, Oberman confirms that until the beginning of the fourteenth century theologians were using the term Tradition to mean Tradition I, while the activity of Tradition II was more or less an addendum.[142]

One of the most important documents in the Late Medieval period is the treatise by John Brevicoxa *De Fide et Ecclesia*. It appears in the work of his Colleague Jean Gerson who, according to Oberman, did not allow due attention for such an important work in the debate between the superiority of Scripture and Tradition (and the distinction between Tradition I and Tradition II). Oberman urges us to investigate this very important

---

[141] Tavard, 22.
[142] Oberman, *The Harvest of Medieval Theology*, 374.

document.[143]

John Brevicoxa's name is absent in the encyclopaedias despite his prestige. Oberman says in summarizing his life: "he entered the foremost Parisian College of Navarre in 1367 to study grammar, philosophy and theology. In 1375 Brevicoxa wrote *A Treatise on Faith, the Church, the Roman Pontiff, and the General Council* for his higher degree. This treatise was divided into three parts, the first establishes the foundations of faith and its concepts; the second part explains the church and its hierarchy; and the final part raises the question "Can the Roman Church err in matters of faith?" He agrees with the "unanimous witness of all scholastics" that the Universal church, in contrast to the Roman Church, cannot err."[144]

Brevicoxa's treatise poses fifteen questions and through the answers he concludes that the content of faith is clear.[145] In his first question he defined Catholic truth as follows:

> Catholic truth is that truth which any pilgrim, of sound mind and having been sufficiently instructed in the Law of Christ, is required to believe either explicitly or implicitly as a condition for salvation.[146]

Another important achievement is that Brevicoxa defines for the

---

[143] H. Oberman, *Forerunners of the Reformation*, 60.
[144] Ibid, 61.
[145] J. Brevicoxa, *A treatise on Faith, the Church, the Roman Pontiff, and the General Council,* quoted in Oberman, *Forerunners of the Reformation*, 68.
[146] Ibid, 68.

first time Tradition I. He argued six proofs in asserting that only truths which are in the Divine Scripture and which can be deduced from Scripture ought to be counted among Catholic truths. The first argument he used was the authority of Solomon "So do not add to his words lest he rebuke you and you be found a liar" (Proverb 30:6). Secondly, he appeals to the authority of Augustine when he wrote "I have learned to give this regard only to those books which are called canonical so that I can firmly believe that no error crept into them as they were being written down. Even if I find something in them which appears to be contrary to the truth, or if I find a corrupt textual tradition, or if the exegesis is not faithful to the actual text or is not clear to me, I do not hesitate in my belief. But I do not have such a regard for other books or writings."[147] Thirdly, Brevicoxa distinguishes the later writings (after the canonical New Testament) and quoting Augustine notes: "The authority of this kind of writing ought to be distinguished from the authority of canonical writings. The former ought not to be read as a determinative witness against which no conflicting theological opinions are permitted." Fourthly, he notes that Augustine, who is as great an authority as any of the biblical writers, testified of himself that no one is required to believe in his writings as a condition for salvation. Fifthly, he confirms that no Catholic truth is found outside the Holy Scripture and quotes Augustine "In Divine Scripture, everything useful is found and

---

[147] The source of this passage is Augustine, *Letter 82.1*, See *Sant'Agostino, Epistolae*. Available [Internet] <http://www.sant-agostino.it/latino/lettere/index2.htm> [9th June 2004].

everything harmful is condemned." And lastly, he rests on the authority of Jerome who says, "An assertion not based on scriptural authority is as easily discarded as it is proved."[148]

Meanwhile he also argues and defends the truths that are not found in the Scripture, or deduced from scripture, but asserted to be a condition of salvation. He states seven reasons to defend them as Tradition II. Firstly, attesting the authority of Innocent III, "although the words of the sacrament of the Holy Eucharist are by no means to be found in their entirety in Scripture, nevertheless we must be firm in our belief that this formula was instituted by Christ." Secondly, he cites the testimony of Pope Agathus who says: "All apostolic injunctions ought to be accepted as if they were uttered by the divine voice of Peter himself." Thirdly, he argues that because the church has such statements as "The Creed was drawn up by the Apostles", "The Petrine See was translated from Antioch to Rome" and "The Roman Popes succeed the blessed Peter" and none of these are in the Holy Scriptures they are true because they are needed for Salvation. Fourthly, he argues that Catholics are bound to believe all doctrinal determinations of the Pope as far as this does not contradict with the will of God. Fifthly, he accords the orally commanded teaching reverence on the same level as the respect of the written word (as both having been taught by Christ and his Apostles). Lastly, he argues that the Universal Church cannot err, since the Truth himself testified "I am with you

---

[148] Brevicoxa, *A treatise on Faith, the Church, the Roman Pontiff, and the General Council*: quoted in Oberman, *Forerunners of the Reformation*, 69-70.

always, to the close of the age" (Matt 28:20).[149]

In spite of his clear definition of the Catholic truth, Brevicoxa causes a great confusion in considering the translation of the Petrine See from Antioch to Rome as a doctrine needed for salvation. Brevicoxa's six proofs for Tradition I are both Orthodox and Patristic. However, it is worth mentioning that the third proof was later denied by Martin Luther when he degraded some of the New Testament writings.[150] Additionally, the fifth and the sixth proofs contradict Brevicoxa's reasons for accepting the existence of Tradition II.

Brevicoxa's seven arguments for Tradition II are very problematic mainly because he considered all articles of Tradition II as essential for salvation. In his first argument, he affirms that the words of the Eucharist are not found entirely in Scripture, but it should be firmly believed that Christ has formulated it, being the sacrament. The Orthodox community believes that the whole Sacrament was instituted by Christ and asserts that the wording of the liturgy was formulated later by the apostles and the Church Fathers except the few word established by Christ himself. The second argument could be accepted only if there are no contradictions with Scripture and with no innovations whatsoever. The third and the fourth arguments are of major importance as they left opened the door for Popes to innovate, add, and omit

---

[149] Ibid, 71-72.
[150] A detailed explanation will be furnished in the next chapter.

whatever they want with the warrant that they are talking with the mouth of Peter. The fifth argument is quite weak because all of what was called oral teaching was written somewhere- either in the Scripture or in other Church books. His last argument about the infallibility of the Church was disproved as the Church strayed and left Scripture and Patristic Tradition behind.

Tavard, in his analysis of the meaning of the Oral tradition and how it was used by theologians from generation to generation, establishes that nothing has reached us through merely oral channels. Everything was written eventually at a certain time. In observing this he adds:

> Neither the Fathers nor the medieval theologians believed that elements of the Apostles' doctrine had been transmitted orally from generation to generation. To their mind, "tradition" is indeed a handing down of the apostolic teaching considered in its totality: whether it was written in Holy Scripture or was later noted down in the "other Scriptures", such a tradition excludes the idea of a purely oral transmission for which there would be no documentary evidence. For the very concept of tradition as being the handing down of something – a cult, a doctrine, a set of inspired writings – implies that each century "received" it though the common activity of the body of Christ: worshipping, baptizing, announcing the message, reading the book in the liturgy. And all nothing essentially "oral" about them: they were acts of fellowship and not esoteric transmission of an

unwritten teaching.[151]

Oberman sees that in the mind of the medieval theologians there was no clear separation between Tradition I and Tradition II. Those who hold Tradition II continue to declare the sufficiency of Holy Scripture. He explains the reason for developing Tradition II:

> Whereas the canon lawyers in the Basilean line are straightforward in positing two sources requiring equal respect, it appears that the scholastic doctors of Scripture develop the oral tradition in a more subtle way. In theory the material sufficiency of Holy Scripture is upheld long after it had been giving up in practice. The key term of this development is the word "implicit", and the history of this term is one of increasing loss of content. When finally the two propositions, "Holy Scripture implicitly says" and "Holy Scripture silently says", are equated, the exegetical concept of Tradition I has fully developed into what we have called Tradition II and the Basilean passage borrowed from canon law provides the rational and patristic authority.[152]

Gabriel Biel[153] discovers in St. Basil the warrant for investing unwritten traditions with the same apostolic authority as Scripture[154]. However, he claims in his comments on the Dominican use of the 1323 canonization of Thomas Aquinas, that the personal sanctity of a doctor of Scripture does not give his

---

[151] Tavard, 56.
[152] Oberman, *Forerunners of the Reformations*, 59.
[153] Biel (1420- 1495) is a German philosopher one of the last great scholastic theologians, follower of Occam. Biel instructed Bartholomaeus Arnoldi von Usingen, who was Luther's teacher at Erfurt. Luther read Biel extensively, for more see Douglas, 132.
[154] Oberman, *Forerunners of The Reformation*, 58.

writings infallibility but it should be tested and compared with Scripture and any conclusions drawn from Scripture.[155]

Tavard finds Biel the chief of the nominalists of his time and a useful embodiment of the perplexity of this era. He finds in some of Biel's quotes the confirmation of Scriptural sufficiency in all aspects needed for the rule of faith. Contrary to this Biel asserts that where such confirmation was not found in the Scripture, the whole church is right to hold it because many other points must be believed (as derived from Christ) outside of what was written.[156] In the same way Biel criticizes the canon lawyers and cautions against the authority of canon law. By way of contrast he stresses that the commands of the Pope have to be obeyed and all papal laws are binding on all the church faithful.[157]

Oberman declares that the unintended view of Biel is that Scripture and Tradition are two distinguishable sources through which revelation flows,[158] Biel asserts that the Church and the Scriptures cannot be set up as rivals, because the Church has ontological priority over the Holy Scripture and its role is to move the faithful towards Scripture.[159] In conclusion, the nominalists Occam, d'Ailly and Gerson adhere to Tradition II, which is extra-scriptural teachings, while at the same time holding to the

---

[155] Oberman, *The Harvest of Medieval Theology*, 394.
[156] Tavard, 62.
[157] Oberman, *The Harvest of Medieval Theology*, 401.
[158] Ibid, 397.
[159] Ibid, 400.

sufficiency of Scripture.[160] Biel believes the same, but to sort this problem out he states that all that the Church believes is Catholic truth.[161]

The Orthodox Church accepts Tradition II as described by Occam, d'Ailly, Gerson and Biel, as far as there is no contradictions with the Scripture. It is quite consistent with an Orthodox way of thinking because it was the theme of Church life throughout its history. This shows, and confirms, that the rise of the tension (calling Scripture and Tradition two different sources of revelation) was alien to Orthodox Patristic understanding.

Humanists such as Johann Wessel of Gansfort (1419-1489) tried to offer another solution to this debate between the Holy Scripture and the Church. Wessel was educated at Deventer under the Brethren of the Common Life. He taught at Heidelberg and then in Paris. He was an able scholar who knew Greek and Hebrew—a scholarly ability that was very unusual at that time. He started as a follower of Thomas Aquinas but changed his views to be Augustinian and later added the nominalist ideas of Occam. He attempted to combine the philosophies of nominalism and mysticism, which gave him the nickname the "Master of Contradictions". He is regarded as a forerunner of the Reformation. Luther edited some of his writings in 1521. He accepted that Christ has real presence at the Eucharist, but he

---

[160] Ibid, 399.
[161] Ibid, 400.

rejected transubstantiation, condemned clerical abuses, papal and conciliar infallibility, asserted that forgiveness is only through God's grace, and affirmed the belief that justification is by faith. Accordingly, also, he denounced indulgences.[162]

Tavard finds that Wessel is not consistent with Luther in holding to the *sola scriptura* principle. He puts greater emphasis on what he called "the rule of faith." Wessel confirms two strands to the rule of faith. First, the Sacred Scripture are not adequate alone as a rule of faith. Second, the unwritten apostolic tradition, which was handed down should be accepted as equal to canonical Scripture in the rule of faith. Later he added a third element and called it the "common consent" which has the right to distinguish between what is acceptable as Tradition and what is to be rejected.[163]

Here we can see Wessel coming closer to the Orthodox Patristic understanding. For Wessel there is one ' rule of faith,' which is 'Tradition' in Orthodox thought. This 'rule of faith' for him is Scripture and apostolic Tradition, while for the Orthodox it is Tradition as a whole, part of which includes Scripture. The 'common consent' for Wessel is equivalent to the Orthodox Church councils which guards the true Tradition to ensure that it is holy without blemish and free from innovations.

---

[162] Douglas, 1035.
[163] Tavard, 69.

Wessel's reply to Hoeck's[164] letter about the indulgences shows in many ways that he accords higher respect to Scripture than to human assertions, regardless of who holds them. At the same time he respects ecclesiastical authority and Catholic truth[165]. Moreover, he defends Gerson- agreeing with him in condemning indulgences and attacking Antoninus the bishop of Florence (who treated anyone who wrote against the indulgences as a heretic).[166] The thrust of this argument was that indulgences are neither mentioned in the Scripture nor handed down through Apostolic Tradition, and there was no observance of this Tradition (without interruption) from apostolic times.[167] Consequently, he rejected indulgences, as for him, it was a patently confused belief—and confused belief cannot be Catholic under any definition of Catholic belief.[168] He explains the famous words of Augustine as such:

> Augustine's statement regarding the relation between the Church and the Gospel does not prove any more than it says: "I would not have believed the Gospel if I had not believed the Church". This statement does not compare the relative authority of Scripture with that of the Church but rather describes how faith begins. Each one who stood in the multitude listening to

---

[164] Jacobus Angularius, born in the first half of the fifteenth century, he got his master of art at Paris. In 1460 was elected to be the rector of the University, and in 1474-1476 was referred as Prior Sorbonnae. Wessel was in Paris and met him from 1458 to 1460 and from 1471 till 1473. Oberman, *Forerunners of the Reformation*, 63.
[165] Wessel, *The Letter in Reply to Hoeck by Wessel Gansfort*, Groningen, September 19, 1489, the whole letter quoted in Oberman, *Forerunners of the Reformation*, 100.
[166] Ibid, 105.
[167] Ibid, 106.
[168] Ibid, 101.

Peter would have said, "I would not have believed the Gospel if I had not believed Peter". Likewise I can say today, "If I, as a boy, had not believed my family and then my teachers and finally the Church, I would never have believed the Gospel today". But I believe the Gospel more than any human multitude and, what is more, I ought to believe it even if I thought everyone else disbelieved it. Even in such case I ought to depend on the Gospel more than on men. Augustine refers in this quotation to the growing faith in a child, not to a comparison of the relative worthiness of the authority of Scripture and that of the Church.[169]

Wessel believes with the Holy Church but he does not believe in the Church because he sees believing as an act of love and a sacrifice which should be offered to God alone. Thus, when he connects belief in the Gospel with belief in God (and for the sake of the Gospel) he believes the Pope as subservient to the Scriptures[170]. He acknowledges the authority of the Pope not because he is the Pope, but because he speaks 'in the Spirit of God'. Finally he says 'We believe in God, not in the Catholic Church, not in the Latin Council, not in the Pope."[171]

Wessel's rejection of indulgences is based on the conditions espoused by St. Vincent of Lérins. For Wessel, indulgences were not taught in the Church always, by all and everywhere. This shows that the Orthodox Patristic measures to

---

[169] Ibid, 11.
[170] Tavard, 69.
[171] Ibid, 70.

canonize or judge any doctrine can be applied in most cases to set up a clear decision in matters of faith. His explanation of Augustine words is more realistic and closer to the Orthodox Patristic understanding. The Orthodox never had the question of who has the supremacy - Scripture or the Church.

Brevicoxa pronounces: "The Universal Church cannot err, since the Truth himself testified, "I am with you always, to the close of the ages (Matt. 28:20), and even prayed that Peter's faith might never fail."[172] Contrary to Brevicoxa, Wessel sees that the Pope can err and that the Church as a whole can err when the power of love is absent, since the unity of the Church is not based on the Pope but on Christ himself. He adds that the task of the church is to safeguard the apostolic faith not to invent new truths, as in the case of the indulgences.[173]

Heresies in the Late Medieval Period

Towards the end of the late medieval period the Western church condemned in an extreme way "heresies" that pitted the authority of Scripture against that of Tradition and the Church in an extreme way.

John Wycliffe (c.1329-1384), was a Yorkshire man who attended Oxford University where he received his Doctorate in Theology in 1372. His talents were useful to John of Gaunt (Duke

---

[172] Brevicoxa, cited in Oberman, *Forerunner of the Reformation*, 72.
[173] Oberman, *Forerunners of the Reformation*, 64.

of Lancaster and the son of Edward III) who summoned him to court (1376-1378).[174] Wycliffe offended the church with his nationalist views, where he encouraged the Parliament, the court, and the people to stop sending the yearly payments to the Pope. These were a burden on the English at that time. He criticized the wealth of the Church and he wrote two treatises in support of the decision of Parliament when they decided that the clergy should not hold high secular offices.[175] Herben sums up Wycliffe's teachings:

> It is necessary to outline, briefly at least, the main teachings of Wycliffe; because it should be known in what his influence upon our Hussitism consisted. He accepted the convention of the Church according to the view expressed by St. Augustine. The Church is not the aggregate of all those who confess it, but of those only whom God predestined to salvation, while those whom He knows in advance to be lost can never be remembers of the true Church of Christ. From that Wycliffe concluded that there is no difference between priest and bishop or between a clergyman in general and a layman. The chosen, predestined layman is the true Son of God, even if he be not consecrated by a bishop. Another of his teachings was that the only authority in matters of faith is the Gospel, and that in the Gospel there is nothing about the veneration of the saints or pictures, that are no masses for the dead, no purgatory, nor the seven sacraments. And because Wycliffe found from what sources the clergy drew their chief power over the laity, he struck at the

---

[174] Douglas, 1064.
[175] J. Herbon, *Huss and His Followers*, (London: Geoffrey Bles, 1926), 39.

> doctrine that a priest could, by some conjuring trick, transform the host into the real body and blood of Christ. According to Wycliffe bread remains ordinary bread even after its consecration by the priest, and only figuratively or sacramentally becomes the body of Christ. Thus Wycliffe opposed the notorious doctrine of transubstantiation, which afterwards played a great role in the Bohemian, German and Swiss reformations.[176]

In connection with the authority of Scripture Douglas asserts that Wycliffe played an important role as a forerunner of the Reformers:

> He has been called "the Morning Star of the Reformation". Certainly his belief that the Bible was the only authoritative guide for faith and practice would substantiate this claim. In other ways he was a proto-protestant. He denied transubstantiation, attacked the institution of the papacy, repudiated indulgences, and wished to have religious orders abolished. Wycliffe's teaching did not have much effect in England. His connection with the Lollards movement is a matter of dispute.[177]

Wycliffe's teachings had three main points, first his theory of "dominion by grace", second his recognition of the Scripture as the sole rule of faith, and thirdly his teaching about the sacraments.[178] Deanesly also gives an insight into Wycliffe's important role when he comments:

---

[176] Ibid, 40, 41.
[177] Douglas, 1064-5.
[178] M. Deanesly, *A History of the Medieval Church 590- 1500*, (London: Methuen & Co., 1925), 229.

Wycliffe had thus thrown overboard the appeal to the visible and historic church as final authority, and he found an alternative one in the written scriptures. The church had always taught that the Bible was the foundation and criterion of discipline and dogma: but Wycliffe held that the appeal to Scripture involved return to a simplified Christian organization like that of the gospels and Acts. There seemed to him an impossible contrast between the Christianity of his own day, with its splendid court at Avignon, and after 1378 at Rome as well, with its rich and business-like bishops and cardinals, and the lives of the fishermen Christians of the gospels. The whole thing was wrong: men ought to follow the "meek and poor and charitable living of Christ," and those who followed it most nearly were the most Christian: those who "contraried it" were anti-Christian, and the worldly popes, the head of the system, who contraried it most of all, were most anti-Christian: they were in fact Anti-Christ.[179]

Wycliffe was excommunicated in 1382 and forced to withdraw to his parish in Lutterworth, where he died eighteen months later from a stroke.[180] In the same year the English King Edward II, married the sister of the King of Bohemia – the emperor Wenzel- the daughter of the late king and emperor Charles IV. As a result of this marriage the two universities of Oxford and Prague came closer to each other. Consequently, Wycliffe theories reached Bohemia, but it was not before the first year of the fourteenth century that his main theological work, the *Trialogus*, reached Prague. The man who became familiar with Wycliffe's

---

[179] Ibid, 231.
[180] Ibid, 234.

philosophical writings and proved himself as Wycliffe's second self was John Huss.[181]

Huss (1373-1415) wrote two remarkable works in Czech at Kozi Hrádek notably his *Postilla* and *About the Church*, in which he asserts that the Church is an indivisible society of human beings predestined to salvation, and that the church administration should be in harmony with the Scripture. He adds that the papacy is of worldly origin, and that both temporal and spiritual authorities, if obdurate in sin, lose their power before God. In these cases he was satisfied that he was right and the Church was in error.[182]

Huss always insisted on the primacy of Scripture and argued that the authority of Sacred Scripture is the first *locus* and any other arguments are subordinate. He was aware of a nuanced origination of Sacred Scripture which he explains as a progression in three senses; first is the Word of God, second is Christ and third is Scriptures given by Christ. This then allows for all available documents that speak about Christ. [183]

At the Council of Constance in 1415 Huss was called to defend forty-five extracts from his works, all considered as heretical. He argued that most of them were detached from their context and some of them were imputed meanings which he never taught or preached. Huss declared in this session "I am ready

---

[181] Hughes, 312.
[182] Herben, 55-6.
[183] Tavard, 50.

humbly to retract anything that shall be proved to me to be erroneous by Scripture"[184].

Herben states that Huss's rejection of unconditional submission to the council and to the Pope was never known before. He considers him the first human being in the Middle Ages to refuse to obey the councils, an act considered as the impudence and obduracy of a heretic. When one of the doctors in attendance said to Huss "Should the Council declare thou hast only one eye, although thou hast two, thou must, like the Council, say it is so." Huss replied "Even if the whole world would say that to me, I , having the reason I have now, could not say such a thing without my conscience contradicting me"[185] Herben comments that Huss caused a conflict in Constance between the old and the new world , between the new ideas about the principles of Christian life where authority lost, and reason and conscience won. That is why Huss is called the torch, which threw light into the medieval darkness[186]. Herben declares:

> Those words were new words in the Church: the reason and the conscience of the individual as against as authority, violent and omnipotent. This is the new idea in which Huss gave to the world, that there is no man under the sun who can, by command, force another either to believe or disbelieve something. The old doctrine of the two swords crumbled into dust. The Pope's hand held

---

[184] Ibid., 57.
[185] Ibid, 59.
[186] Ibid, 62.

teaching, the Emperor's the compelling sword. But they neither taught nor compelled Huss to do anything that against his reason and conscience. [187]

The rise of all biblicist heresies occurred after the Great Schism, where the Scripture was not read in the Church, or read only in Latin which most people could not understand. The main reasons for these so-called heresies were the innovations of major non-biblical teachings such as purgatory, indulgences, the Immaculate Conception of the Virgin Mary. Such innovations affect the meaning of the salvation and make God's grace very cheap and even of no use.

Peter d'Ailly, who voted for Huss' death in Constance,[188] shared with him his protest against the Canon law teachers, who receive their own decrees as though they were divine Scriptures.[189] Gerson, who did the same at Constance, sees that Huss did not make differentiation between the Tradition of the first five centuries and later traditions. Gerson acknowledges the importance of the doctors of Scriptures and gives the impression that there is a real doctoral succession.[190] On other occasions he joined with him in the attack on the curialistic position, which was directed mainly against the extreme canonists, leading him to stress the contrast between human traditions and divine law.[191]

---

[187] Ibid, 61.
[188] Ibid, 60
[189] Tavard, 54
[190] Oberman, *The Harvest of Medieval Theology*, 390
[191] Ibid, 379

Conclusion

The Great Schism between the West and the East seems to have been a turning point in the West. After the Schism, the West began to develop a different and less coherent understanding of Holy Tradition than that which prevailed in the East. Konstantinidis argues:

> The second aspect of Tradition within the Church is that which begins with the manifestation of the historical division of the Church into Eastern and Western Churches, as we are accustomed to say. Two different types of tradition have been formed under different local and temporal limits. These are the "differentiated Traditions of the East and the West". And so the subject Traditions appears, once more, as a clear ecclesiological theme; the divided Church appears in divided Tradition, and this dichotomized Tradition corresponds to a Church divided in itself.[192]

The Western church began to try to *develop* tradition, and this development led many Western theologians to regard Scripture, Tradition and Church as separate sources of authority rather than in terms of a single *Paradosis* and this led to the Reformation dilemma in which the two sides attempted to claim supremacy for either Tradition/Church or Scripture.

The late medieval period saw many innovated doctrines in the Roman Catholic Church. Such doctrines were clear deviations from the One Holy Tradition of the Orthodox Patristic Church.

---

[192] Konstantinidis, 225

Since the Churches separated officially in 1054 doctrines such as Celibacy enforced for priests and presbyters by Pope Gregory VII (1079), Rosary beads which were innovated by Peter the Hermit (1090), Sales of indulgences (1090), Baptism by sprinkling accepted as the universal standard instead of immersion for all, not just the sick (Council of Ravenna, 1311) and purgatory (the Council of Florence, 1439) have arisen which have never been believed in the Orthodox Patristic Tradition. The major innovations which caused the problems and hinders unifications are purgatory, indulgences, Immaculate Conception of Virgin Mary and the Supremacy of the Pope as a condition for salvation.

Such innovations distracted and disturbed the daily life of the Church and caused unrest and instability in the Western Church. Accordingly, many started to rebel and object to such innovations. Tavard finds that the unsettled relation between the Church and Scripture at the end of the fourteenth century lead to a big question: "Could the Western Church in the fifteenth and the sixteenth centuries, caught in the whirlwind of the theological decadence, to be restored to the pattern of Orthodoxy?"[193] He summarizes the dilemma of the fifteenth century:

> The basic dilemma of the fifteenth century resides in this struggle between the traditional and theological conception of Scripture as the backbone of the Church's authority and the canonistic pressure for sharper and sharper

---

[193] Tavard, 43.

affirmation and practice of the primacy of the Pope.[194]

A fitting answer to the question raised at the end of the fourteenth century and the dilemma of the fifteenth century was voiced by Nicholas de Clemanges who appealed for the establishment of General Councils where the church could determine her faith. He doubted that such Councils would restrict themselves to matters that strictly pertain to faith and in this he was proved correct. He did not trust these Councils as he saw them erring because of the lack of study of the divine Scripture and the writings of the Church Fathers.[195]

Oberman and Tavard see the papacy's attempt to assert its power through the "traditions" of canon law in opposition to what it is perceived as threats to the Church from European rulers and the Conciliarist movement. They held that a Council of the Church had higher authority than the Pope.

In the midst of this debate the forerunners of the Reformation appeared. They rejected the idea that the letters and all papal traditions have the same authority as the gospel. Also they rejected the idea that the Pope grants dispensations against the Apostles and is empowered to correct the gospels.[196] In general they accepted Tradition I, but they rejected Tradition II. They discarded Tradition II mainly because of the more recent

---

[194] Tavard, 49.
[195] Tavard, 55-56.
[196] Wycliffe, C. II, Vol. I, p. 34 quoted in Tavard, 41.

innovations and the unclear definition of it at that time. Oberman puts Wycliffe, Huss and Wessel Gansfort as exponents of Tradition I against tradition II who never accepted the supremacy of Tradition in relation to Scripture[197]. The Orthodox Church thinks these changes took place in the West in the Middle Ages leading "heretical" figures like Huss and Wycliffe to pit the authority of Scripture against that of the Church for the first time. Consequently, this attitude and these circumstances paved the way for the Reformation and to the concept of *sola scriptura*.

---

[197] Oberman, *Forerunners of the Reformation*, 59.

4 LUTHER ON *SOLA SCRIPTURA* AND TRADITION

The purpose of this Chapter is to map the gradual rise of the tension between Scripture and Tradition in the mind of Martin Luther which led him to adopt *sola scriptura*. It shows also what Luther has recaptured from the late medieval theologians and the forerunners of the Reformation. Furthermore, it investigates Luther's views in the light of the Orthodox Patristic standpoint which was explained in the first chapter.

The main works investigated in this chapter are *The Leipzig Disputation* (1519) and *On Councils and the Church* (1539). Some other works like *Table-Talk* and The *Schmalkaldic Articles* (1536) will be quoted to help in this investigation. The Chapter begins with the different views of some theologians commenting on Luther's works in understanding the relation between Scripture and Tradition. The meanings of the words: Fathers, Councils, Church and Tradition in this chapter are those meant by Luther. Accordingly, a special attention will be given to the role of the Fathers and the authority of the councils.

An historical background for the *Leipzig Disputation* and *On Councils and the Church* is furnished to show the importance of and the circumstances in which such works were born. In addition an analysis of the aftermath of each of them is given.

The conclusion of this chapter will examine how far Luther conformed to the Orthodox Patristic views of Tradition and to what extent he deviated from it. It will show fairly what has been reformed in the Western Church because of such return to the original meaning of the Tradition. However, it will demonstrate how Luther opened a door (without any limitation) to deparentify[198] the Fathers leading to some canonized books being degraded or rejected.

Scholars' Overview

The Leipzig debate was considered of great importance in the life of the Reformation and also in the development of the *sola scriptura* principle. In the *Career of the Reformer* Pelikan says:

> The Leipzig debate is of great significance in Luther's development as a reformer primarily because he on that occasion publicly stated his evangelical conception of the church in unmistakable terms and showed that in the last analysis his sole authority in matters of faith was the Word of God. Therefore he could state without reservation that not only the papacy but also church councils could err. This made reconciliation with Roman church virtually impossible. It led inexorably to the threat of excommunication and finally excommunication

---

[198] This is a term borrowed from studies of Family Therapy and it will be justified and expounded upon in detail in the conclusion of this chapter.

itself.[199]

Lohse notes that Rome played a major part in this controversy and compelled Luther to fall back on to *sola scriptura*:

> In the course of his dispute with Rome he was forced more and more to give Scripture critical value against specific traditions and doctrinal opinions in tension with or actually opposed to Scripture.[200]

It is easy to accept the claims of Pelikan and Lohse, as Luther himself did not intend to establish a new Church. Initially Luther felt that by declaring his Ninety-nine theses, he would reform Church teachings from within and would do a favor to the Pope himself. A closer look to the sequence of the events after posting the Ninety-five theses shows clearly that the arrogance of the Church and especially Eck in his responses to Luther (as will be illustrated later in this chapter). This led to a wider gap between Scripture and Church. Subsequently, Luther believed that he represented the Church because he held Scripture and this led to his excommunication later in January 1521.

Sproul argues that the chief theological issue for the Reformation was the matter of Justification. This strongly undermined the underlying question of Authority and led to the

---

[199] Luther, Martin. *Luther's Works, Vol. 31: Career of the Reformer I*, edited by :J. J. Pelikan, H. C. Oswald & H. T. Lehmann, , [CD ROM] Philadelphia: Fortress Press, 1999, 311 . For simplification in all other footnotes from the same [CD ROM], I will use (LW, Vol. No., p No.).
[200] Bernhard Lohse, eds. and trans. by Roy Harrisville, *Martin Luther's Theology: Its Historical and Systematic Development*. (Edinburgh: T&T Clark, 1999), 187.

principle of *sola scriptura*.[201] Agreeing with Sproul is easier than disagreeing with him, as Luther made it clear later that a Church Father cannot be ranked as a Doctor of the Church[202] unless he wrote and taught about justification. However, Luther sometimes used an unbalanced stance against the Fathers and attacked them unfaithfully. He denied all their efforts and teachings, sometimes for not writing about justification and other times with no clear reason. A clear example of such an attack is his words in the *Table-talk* quoted later in this chapter.

Lohse in his analysis affirms that Luther agreed with Huss's statement that it is not necessary for salvation to believe that the Roman Church is superior to the other churches.[203] In addition to that in his comments on the effect of the Leipzig disputation on Luther he says:

> Luther was not content with accepting as Christian and evangelical only a few of the articles of Huss condemned at Constance. On the basis of continually developing contacts with Bohemian theologians, and after reading some writings by Huss, he recognized that in all essential questions Huss had taught "evangelically" and for it suffered a martyr's death. Luther's evaluation of the Hussites thus soon came to be more positive than at Leipzig. Criticism of them receded altogether. As early as in his June 1520 treatise, *To the Christian nobility of the German Nation*, he urged serious

---

[201] R.C. Sproul, eds. by James Boice, *The foundation of Biblical Authority,s* (London, Glasgow: Pickering & Inglis, 1978), 103.
[202] More detail is given later in this chapter.
[203] Lohse, 123.

discussions with the Bohemians with aim of possibly overcoming division of the Bohemians in surprisingly cautious and discrete fashion[204].

It is worth mentioning here that Luther used the Eastern Orthodox Church as an example to defend his point of view. In the Leipzig debate Luther avers that neither the Greek Church nor the ancient Fathers were under the Roman pontiff.[205] For nearly a thousand years the Latin Church did not claim that the Greek had lost their salvation. Here Luther was reaffirming the old position of the Orthodox Tradition in this regard and the rejection of the Roman Catholic innovation of the primacy of Rome over the whole Church in the world. He did not necessarily want to affirm other Orthodox positions. His use of this is mainly strategic-he's pointing out that the Roman Church doesn't deny that the "Greeks" are Christian, even though they don't accept the authority of the pope.

The author of the essay *"Deparentifying the Fathers"* Scott Hendrix says that the position of most of the reformers was: "when the Fathers speak, they should be tested by the canon of the Scriptures." If they are not in agreement with Scripture, they should either be rejected or clarified with glosses.[206]

According to Luther, "Where the gospel is not preached

---

[204] Ibid, 125.
[205] L W, Vol. 31, 322.
[206] Hendrix, S. "Deparentifying the Fathers: The Reformers and Patristic Authority." In *Tradition and Authority in the Reformation,* ed. L. Grane, A., Schindler and M. Wried, (Asgate: Variorum, 1996), 60.

there is no Church"[207] and "Where the gospel is rightly and purely preached, there a holy, Christian Church must be."[208] He continues in a similar vein and says, "Where the gospel is preached, there this star shines upright, there without a doubt Christ is present."[209] For Luther, the absence of the Scripture is the absence of Christ, and in the absence of Christ there is complete darkness.

Pelikan confirms that, for Luther, the general councils of the Church could err. For him, Constance erred when it condemned certain teachings of Huss.[210] He adds that this forced Luther to admit publicly that some articles of Huss, which were condemned in Constance, were truly Christian.[211] Consequently, this admission at the Leipzig Debate in 1519 made both Luther and his opponents begin to be aware of the estrangement between him and the Roman Church.[212] This stand of Luther was a protest against the errors of the Catholic Church in Constance on the one hand and a return to the Orthodox teaching in the concerned points of protest on the other hand. But here Luther claims that any general council of the church can err-not just Constance. Thus, in principle, even one of the first seven councils of the church could err. This isn't consistent with the Orthodox position, which holds that genuine general councils (i.e. the first seven) cannot err

---

[207] L W, Vol. 32, *In Defense and Explanation of All the Articles*, 73.
[208] L W, Vol. 38, *Private Mass and the Consecration of Priests*, 211.
[209] L W, Vol. 52, *The Gospel for the Festival of the Epiphany*, 275.
[210] Jaroslav Pelikan, *Obedient Rebel: Catholic Substance and Protestant Principle in Luther's Reformation*. (SCM Press LTD, London) 1964, 54.
[211] Ibid, 120.
[212] Ibid, 54.

because they are organs of the Tradition.

How the Debate Took Place

After Luther posted his Ninety-five theses in 1517, a series of debates, correspondences, charges, and counter charges ensued, concluding in Luther's dramatic insistence in *sola scriptura*. In the summer of 1519 the debate between Luther and Johannes von Eck took place at Leipzig. The relation between Eck and Luther began as a friendly exchange of letters early in 1517. But in less than a year Eck suddenly broke his friendship with Luther by the publication of his *Obelisks*, in which he attacked thirty-one theses of Luther's ninety-five theses in very abusive language. Luther answered him with his vehement *Asterisks* in March 1518.[213]

Eck did not reply to Luther's *Asterisks*, assuming that the polemics would end at this point. However Carlstadt, who was the dean of the Theological faculty at Wittenberg University at that time, felt that he had to defend the situation of his colleague, so he wrote 370 theses in its defence. Subsequently Eck expressed his regret, as he considered Carlstadt had gone too far and Eck asked Carlstadt to drop the controversy. This request came too late because Carlstadt's theses had been already published. Finally, Luther, Carlstadt, and Eck agreed to hold the disputation in Leipzig.[214]

---

[213] Ibid, 307.
[214] Ibid, 307, 311.

Luther was surprised when he received a copy of Eck's theses towards the end of January 1519. He discovered that the challenge was for him and not for Carlstadt. Eck wrote twelve theses. Eleven of them dealt with indulgences and the twelfth was a defence of the papal supremacy and a direct attack on Luther's explanation of thesis twenty-two. Luther considered himself relieved from his promise to Miltitz [215] to discontinue the indulgences controversy, as his opponents had not done the same.[216]

Luther in his letter [217] to Spalatin [218] mentioned how the bishop of Merseburg tried to inhibit the debate and fixed a notice at the doors of the churches that the debate should not be held, this *Inhibition* was accompanied with the newly published explanations of the papal decree on indulgences of November 9, 1518. Apparently a copy of this decretal had been sent to Bishop Adolph of Merseburg who believed that this decretal had decided the questions for debate.[219] But this *Inhibition* was disregarded, and the man who posted it was jailed by the city council, as he had not got a permission to do so.

---

[215] Miltitz, Carl (1490-1529) papal secretary and sub nuncio to Germany, see Douglas, 661.
[216] L W, Vol. 31, 311.
[217] Letter dated July 20, 1519.
[218] Spalatin (1482-1545) is a German Reformer attended universities of Erfurt and Wittenberg. In 1508 became the tutor to the future elector John Fredrick. His friendship to Fredrick and Luther was of great influence to the Reformation, see Douglas, 924.
[219] L W, Vol. 31, 318.

Schaff states that the disputation was held in the large hall of the castle Pleissenburg at Leipzig under the sanction of Duke George of Saxony. He describes it as one of the great intellectual battles between Carlstadt and Luther on one side and Eck on the other side. They debated the doctrines of the papal primacy, free will, good works, purgatory, and indulgences. The disputation lasted for nearly three weeks. The first act was the disputation between Eck and Carlstadt, on the freedom of the human will which was denied by Carlstadt and affirmed by Eck. The second and more important act began on July 4, between Eck and Luther on the primacy of the Pope.[220] Melanchthon attended with Luther, as a spectator suggesting to him and Carlstadt occasional arguments, and hereafter stood by Luther as his faithful colleague and friend.[221]

Leipzig Debate

In spite of the fact that the main subject of the debate was the indulgences (dealt with in the first twelve of Eck's theses and expected to be highly controversial) it was noted that they were quite peacefully discussed. However, the thirteenth thesis, which Eck had added, became the heated debate. This reads:

> The very callous decrees of the Roman pontiffs, which have appeared in the last four hundred years, prove that the Roman church is superior to all others. Against them stand the history of

---

[220] Schaff, Vol. 7, 144-145.
[221] Ibid, 147.

eleven hundred years, the test of divine Scripture, and the decree of the Council of Nicaea, the most sacred of all councils.[222]

Luther started his debate by attacking Eck, describing him as dedicated to the Apostolic See and the Church. He explained that the word 'Church' meant Eck's own opinions and those of his heroes. Furthermore, he considered it a good opportunity to answer the blasphemies of Eck once and for all. He accused Eck of having lost his skills to the extent that he and his followers could not correctly understand correctly the good things they had learned.[223]

Eck vilified Luther as a heretic and 'Bohemian'; on the ground that Luther had asserted that among the articles of Huss was one that stated that the pre-eminence of the papacy came from the emperor. Here he cited Platina[224]:

> I, however, undertook to prove that this power was derived, not from imperial, but from papal decrees. The Lateran Church itself in an inscription sings about the origin and the extent of its authority, stating that by papal and imperial decrees it is the mother of churches etc.[225]

Luther replied that these little verses he refers to are well-known

---

[222] L W, Vol. 31, 318
[223] Ibid, 311.
[224] Bartolomeo Platina (1421–1481), a humanist librarian of Sixtus IV who continued the account of the old *Liber pontificalis* or collection of biographies of the popes to 1471.
[225] L W, Vol. 31, 315.

verses which express the headship of the Church of Rome. Luther had in his mind that the Roman Church is called by papal decrees and imperial dogmas as the mother and head of all churches.[226]: The inscription was in front of the Lateran Basilica in Rome.[227] As a result Luther found it necessary for Eck to hear that the Church itself should be Hussite in this regard and thus he rekindled the old ashes.

Luther presented himself as a defender of the Christian grace against all Sylvesters[228], Civesters, Cajetans[229], and Ecks.[230] And he declares boldly:

> I am convinced that the Apostolic See neither wills nor can do anything against Christ. Furthermore, in this matter I fear neither the pope nor the name of the pope, much less those little popes and puppets.[231] One thing only am I concerned about, namely, that the despoiling of my Christian name does not bring with it the loss of the most holy doctrine of Christ. In this matter I do not want anyone to expect patience of me. I do not want Eck to look for modesty either under

---

[226] *Dogmate Papali datur et simul Imperiali Quod sim cunctarum Mater, Caput Ecclesiarum.* WA 2, 159, n. 2 cited in Ibid, 315.
[227] Ibid, 315.
[228] Luther here refers to Sylvester Mazzolini ("Prierias") (1456-1523), a Dominican scholar advisor to the Pope, and grand inquisitor; "Civester" is a fictitious name used in a play on words to make this seem ridiculous, footnote in L W, Vol. 31, 317.
[229] Cajetan (1464-1534) is a Dominican cardinal and philosopher. His greatest disappointment was his failure to persuade Luther to recant when he met on three successive days in Augsburg in 1518. Cajetan was one of Luther's most competent opponents, see Douglas, 174 .
[230] LW, Vol. 31, 317.
[231] This is a play on the Latin words *pappos et puppas*.

the black or under the white hood.[232] May the praise of that impious forbearance be damned which was shown by Ahab when he set free Benhadad, the enemy of Israel [I Kings 20].[233]

Hendrix asserts the same; that even prior to Leipzig, Luther was pronounced guilty because of his association with Huss. He notes that this indicated that Luther's battle over the indulgences was only superficially what the debate was about; the fundamental disagreement being the issue of the nature of the church and its ecclesiastical authority. Hendrix adds that Eck cited the three proposition of Huss, which had been condemned at the council of Constance. First, that Peter never was the head of the Catholic Church, secondly, there is no evidence that there is one head to govern the church and thirdly, the popes owed their origin to the emperors. Consequently, Eck citied the bull *Unam sanctam* (1302) of Boniface VIII: "It is necessary to salvation for every human creature to be submissive to the Roman pontiff."[234]

Eck was naïve in his arguments regarding the primacy of Peter, to the extent that he interprets the Scripture in his own way. He saw in Peter walking on the water a proof of his rule over the world, as for him the water symbolizes the world. Luther mentioned this strange interpretation of Eck in the *Table-talk* later

---

[232] The Augustinians wore the black hood, while the white by the Dominicans. Eck had previously stated that he had expected more wisdom and patience under a black hood.
[233] L W, Vol. 31, 316.
[234] Citied in Scott Hendrix, "We are all Hussites? Huss and Luther revisited", *Archiv für Reformationsgeschichte 65*. Gütersloh, (1974), 138-139.

in 1533.[235]

Eck has considered Luther's use of the Greek Fathers and the independence of the Eastern Church from Rome -as an example- equivalent to the attack on papal supremacy. Eck described this as a heresy in itself, claiming that Luther and the Bohemians wished to understand Scriptures better than the Church Fathers. Eck mocked him by saying "It would be amazing that God has hidden that truth from so many saints and martyrs prior to the coming of the 'Reverend Father Luther'.[236] As Hendrix notes, Luther's Catholic opponents considered the attack upon the Fathers tantamount to confirm that the Holy Spirit had deserted the Church and deceived the faithful.[237]

Later in a letter to Spalatin, Luther explained how he had refuted all Eck's theses concerning indulgences. Luther mentioned that if he had not questioned the authority of the Pope, the whole debate would have had different results:

> The debate over indulgences fell completely flat, for Eck agreed with me in nearly all respects and his former defence of indulgences came to appear like mockery and derision, whereas I had hoped that this would be the main topic of the debate. He finally acknowledged his position in public sermons so than even the common people could see that he was not concerned with indulgences. He also is supposed to have said that if I had not

---

[235] L W, Vol. 54, 196.
[236] Hendrix, 139-140.
[237] Ibid, 282-283.

questioned the power of the pope, he would readily have agreed with me in all matters.[238]

To clarify Luther's opinion in understanding the Scripture, I will advance to his work *The Bondage of the Will* where he affirms many times that the Scriptures are clear and not obscure. He declares that the Bible can be interpreted by anyone and even by a child of nine years old. He sees no need for the Fathers' interpretation, as there is no book on earth more plainly written than the Holy Scripture. Luther adds in Article XXXVI:

> Peter also saith, (2 Pet. i. 19,) "And we certainly have more surely the word of prophecy; unto which, ye do well that ye take heed, as unto a light shining in a dark place." Here Peter makes the Word of God a clear lamp, and all other things darkness: whereas, we make obscurity and darkness of the Word. Christ also often calls Himself, the "light of the world;" (John viii. 12. ix. 5,) and John the Baptist, a "burning and a shining light," (John v. 35.) Certainly, not on account of the holiness of his life, but on account of the word which he ministered. In the same manner Paul calls the Philippians shining "lights of the world." (Phil. ii. 15), because (says he,) ye "hold forth the word of life." (16) For life without the word is uncertain and obscure. And what is the design of the apostles in proving their preaching by the Scriptures? Is it that they may obscure their own darkness by still greater darkness? What was the intention of Christ, in teaching the Jews to "search the Scriptures" (John v. 39,) as testifying of Him?

---

[238]L W, Vol. 31, 322.

Was it that He might render them doubtful concerning faith in Him? What was *their* intention, who having heard Paul, searched the Scriptures night and day, "to see if these things were so?" (Acts xvii. 11.) Do not all these things prove that the Apostles, as well as Christ Himself, appealed to the Scriptures as the most clear testimonies of the truth of their discourses? With what face then do we make them 'obscure?'[239]

But Luther explained further what he means by such clarity in Article XXXIV in *The Bondage of the Will*. He adds two new terms "external judgment" and "internal judgment":

> We hold the case thus: that the spirits are to be tried and proved by a twofold judgment. The one, internal; by which, through the Holy Spirit, or a peculiar gift of God, any one may illustrate, and to a certainty, judge of, and determine on, the doctrines and sentiments of all men, for himself and his own personal salvation concerning which it is said. (1 Cor. ii. 15.) "The spiritual man judgeth all things, but he himself is judged of no man." This belongs to faith, and is necessary for every, even private, Christian. This, we have above called, 'the internal clearness of the Holy Scripture.' And it was this perhaps to which *they* alluded, who, in answer to you said, that all things must be determined by the judgment of the Spirit. But this judgment cannot profit another, nor are we speaking of this judgment in our present discussion; for no one, I think, doubts its reality.
> The other, then, is the external judgment; by which, we judge, to the greatest certainty, of the

---

[239] Luther, *The bondage of the Will.* Available [Internet] <http://www.covenanter.org/Luther/Bondage/Bowexord.htm> [18th March 2004]

spirits and doctrines of all men; not for ourselves only, but for others also, and for their salvation. This judgment is peculiar to the public ministry of the Word and the external office, and especially belongs to teachers and preachers of the Word. Of this we make use, when we strengthen the weak in faith, and when we refute adversaries. This is what we before called, 'the external clearness of the Holy Scripture.' Hence we affirm that all spirits are to be proved in the face of the church, by the judgment of Scripture. For this ought, above all things, to be received, and most firmly settled among Christians: - that the Holy Scriptures are a spiritual light by far more clear than the sun itself, especially in those things which pertain unto salvation or necessity.[240]

On February 16, 1546, two days before his death, Luther wrote that understanding the Holy Scripture needs more experience and years to grasp. It is not a contradiction to what he said in *The Bondage of the Will*, but it is an affirmation of the need for Fathers, scholars and theologians for external judgment:

> Nobody can understand Vergil in his *Bucolics* and *Georgics*[241] unless he has first been a shepherd or a farmer for five years. Nobody understands Cicero[242] in his letters unless he has been engaged in public affairs of some consequence for twenty years. Let nobody suppose that he has tasted the Holy Scriptures sufficiently unless he has ruled

---

[240] Ibid.
[241] Vergil was the greatest of the Latin poets (70–19 B.C.); his *Bucolics* are poems about the life of shepherds and his *Georgics* are poems about agriculture and farmers. Footnote in L W, Vol. 54, 476.
[242] M. Tullius Cicero (106–43 B.C.), eloquent Roman orator and statesman, was a model of Latin style. Ibid, 222.

over the churches with the prophets for a hundred years. Therefore there is something wonderful, first, about John the Baptist; second, about Christ; third, about the apostles.[243]

In other words he means that any person may interpret the Scripture for him/ herself for personal benefit and understanding but not to form a Church doctrine. Any person with the Spirit may understand them clearly. However, not everyone has the Spirit and not everyone who has the Spirit is strong in faith. For this reason the Church also needs a ministry of the Word to strengthen the weak and refute the enemies of the truth. Luther refuses to identify this ministry with the See of Rome in an exclusive way or to concede that the ministry of the Word is somehow above the Word. Nevertheless there is a teaching ministry that serves the Word and it is here that room left for Oberman's Tradition I. Where Tradition I is the ministry of the Word across the course of history, as explained in chapter II.

Luther contracted Tradition I in a way which allows him to choose from the Fathers what he believed was Scriptural. Through this theological freedom he rejected all the Catholic innovations and cleared the Church from non-Orthodox Patristic teaching. Such acts made him closer to the Orthodox Tradition in one side. On the other hand, he ignored some other Orthodox Patristic interpretations that did not suit his particular theological

---

[243] L W, Vol. 54, *Table Talk*, no. 5677, 476.

understanding. Additionally, he closed the door totally on any extra-scriptural teachings. This dragged him away from the Orthodox Tradition.

On Councils and the Church

Before discussing this work of Luther, I would like to introduce Jaroslav Pelikan and what he discovered as key to understanding the Councils in the mind of Luther. Pelikan asserts that, for Luther, every council has one primary concern, one principal doctrine for the sake of which it was assembled. The same council has some other temporary and external peripheral decisions. He explains this key through the example of the first council in Acts. He finds that the primary concern for this council was not to burden the converted Gentiles to Christianity with any unnecessary yokes. The other fourfold decision had to be seen only on the light of this primary concern.[244] Luther in describing the primary and secondary concerns of the Council of Nicaea and Council in Jerusalem says:

> Thus we see that this council dealt primarily with the article that Christ was truly God, for which it was convoked and for which it is and is called a council. They also dealt with several nonessential, physical, external, temporal matters on the side, rightfully to be viewed as temporal and not to be compared with articles of faith; nor are they to be regarded as eternal law (for they are past and expired). But the council found it necessary to attend to such physical matters as were pertinent and needful in their time, which no longer concern us today, and which are neither possible

---
[244] Pelikan, 74,75.

nor profitable for us to observe. And in proof of this, the article prescribing the rebaptism of heretics is false and wrong, even if it was formulated by the true fathers themselves and not patched together by the Arians or the other loose bishops. Thus the apostolic council in Jerusalem also found it necessary for their day to settle, after it had disposed of the important business, several nonessential, external articles, such as that dealing with blood, strangled animals, and the sacrifice to idols; but not with the intention of making this an eternal law in the church, to be kept as an article of faith, for it has fallen into disuse. And why should we not also examine how this council can be understood within the context of the reasons that made it necessary?[245]

In response to this, Orthodox theologians can agree partially that every Council has its primary concern. Some councils, like Constantinople, had three main concerns to defend the articles of faith. But in many cases the secondary articles are eternal and carry the same importance as the primary ones. Even in the case of the Council of Jerusalem, the Orthodox view the fourfold prohibition as eternal and believe that it will remain eternal. Of course decrees like elevating the see of Constantinople above other sees or to call the bishop of Constantinople a Patriarch [246] are external, temporal, and empirical works.[247]

The meaning of the Church and its nature preoccupied the mind of Luther through-out his life. The editors of Volume 41 of

---

[245] L W, Vol. 41, 68.
[246] Ibid, 89.
[247] Ibid, 91.

his works show that most of his later doctrine of the Church can be found in his treatises on Psalms (1513-1515).[248] They assert that modern studies have modified but not discredited this opinion. They found also that Augustine had influenced him, which can be observed from Luther's marginal notes in *The City of God*.[249]

One of Luther's dreams was for a free Christian Council to define the Church, its doctrines and to forbid all papal innovations. After his meetings with Cajetan in 1518, he appealed to have a general council to express his views on the fallibility of the council of Constance. After the Leipzig disputation and the Diet of Worms, his dreams evaporated. He felt that even if a council would be held the main purpose would be to condemn and excommunicate the Reformers. Thus he wrote his treatises *On the Councils and the Church* (1539) after he had read church history. He begins his treatise by rejecting the Church Fathers in the hope of promoting reformed teachings. He sees the Fathers as mass of contradictions which Scripture should judge at all times. Luther then discussed at length the Christological Councils of the early Church.[250] Here he asserts the Church is primarily the people and reflects on the importance of the doctrine of the Word that "God's Word cannot be without God's people, and conversely, God's people cannot be without God's word." [251] Luther doesn't think of

---

[248] They are referring here to, Karl Holl, "*Luther und die Schwärmer,*" in *Gesammelte Aufsätze zur Kirchengeschichte* (6th ed.; 3 vols.; Tübingen, 1928–1932), I, 288–325.
[249] Gordon Rupp in the introduction to L W Vol. 41, xiii.
[250] Ibid, xiii-xiv.
[251] L W, Vol. 41, 150.

Scripture in isolation. There is never Scripture without the Church. Even though the Church is not above Scripture, and even though the Church is the people of God rather than the clerical hierarchy, Scripture is always oriented towards the Church which the proclamation of the Gospel calls into being. He sees the Church as a Spiritual body "The church is a high, deep, hidden thing which one may neither perceive nor see, but must grasp only by faith, through baptism, sacrament, and word." [252]

Luther wrote *On the Councils and the Church* to present his final judgment concerning the medieval church as well as the primary broad base for a new doctrine of the church within the newly born Lutheranism. Luther introduces his critique of papal and conciliar authority in three parts. The editor of Volume 41 of his works sums them as follows:

> Part I argues that the church cannot be reformed according to the decrees of the councils and the church fathers. Part II discusses the historical significance of the apostolic council at Jerusalem (Acts 15) and the first four ecumenical councils— Nicaea (325), Constantinople (381), Ephesus (431), and Chalcedon (451). Luther concludes from his analysis that although councils protect the church from error, they have no authority to create new articles of faith. Part III deals with the true marks of the church according to Holy Scripture. Luther's earlier proposal at the Leipzig Debate in 1519 that pope and council be made subject to the word of God becomes an elaborate

---

[252] Ibid, 211.

argument for a radically new concept of the church.[253]

In Luther's defence he declared that he read the Fathers with greater diligence than those who quoted them against him so defiantly and haughtily. He accused his opponents of not reading the Holy Scripture, and he advised them to read it and then seek the glosses of the Father and not to ignore any of them. He gave weight to the Fathers, foremost when he worked on the letter of the Hebrews with St. John Chrysostom's commentary, the letter of Titus and to the Galatians with the help of St. Jerome, the Psalter with all the writers available, and so on. He asserts many times that his accusers are too far from the truth when they blamed him for not reading the Fathers.[254]

Meanwhile, he asserted that the Fathers were occasionally very human, and had not overcome the weakness described in the seventh chapter of Romans (Rom 7:7-24). He invoked the words of St. Augustine in his reply to Jerome who was furious because St. Augustine disapproved of one point in his commentary on Galatians where he says "Dear brother (for he was such a fine, friendly man), I hope that you do not expect your books to be regarded as equal to those of the apostles and prophets." He used another quote from a letter [255] to St. Jerome by St. Augustine in

---

[253] L W, Vol. 41, 5.
[254] Ibid, 19-20.
[255] I could not find the same wording in the available translations but similar meanings are in *Letter (28) from Augustine to Jerome*, Ch. III, Article 4. Available

which he says "I have learned to hold the Scriptures alone inerrant. Therefore I read all the others, as holy and learned as they may be; with reservation that I regard their teaching true only if they can prove their statements through Scripture or reason."[256] In the same way he used the analogy of St. Bernard,[257] who learned the wisdom from the trees, such as oaks and pines, he adds that he regards the holy fathers highly but as brooks not as the spring itself. Thus Luther says:

> Scripture, too must remain master and judge, for when we follow the brooks too far, they lead us too far away from the spring, and lose both their taste nourishment, until they lose themselves in the salty sea, as happened under the papacy.[258]

Scott Hendrix argues in *"Deparentifying the Fathers"* that the Reformers, and specifically Luther, adopted an intentionally balanced stance towards the Fathers. They argue that the intention of Luther in picking up from the Fathers some of their sayings was not to serve his own self-interest. They confirmed that the selective use of the Fathers was a result of the theological freedom he had. Such a balanced stance enabled them to acknowledge the Fathers contributions and limitations at the same time. In all cases Luther

---

[Internet] <http://www.newadvent.org/fathers/1102028.htm> [19th March 2004].
[256] L W, Vol. 41, 25-27.
[257] Bernard of Clairvaux (1090–1153), Benedictine abbot and famed mystic. This passage could not be located in Bernard's works. On Luther's attitude toward Bernard, see Walther Köhler, *Luther und die Kirchengeschichte nach Seinen Schriften* (Erlangen, 1900), 320–333, footnote in: L W, Vol. 41, 20.
[258] Ibid, 19-20.

accepted the Fathers contributions as a limited authority beneath Scripture,[259] they add:

> Accordingly, affirmed Luther, they had strong contributions to make to live under the gospel. When the spirit was ruling what they said and did, then their words and deeds were to be gathered up like fragments of the gospel (*fragmenta Evangelica*) i.e. as words and deeds which Christ himself produced in them. Where, however that old adversary the flesh influenced their thoughts and actions, they were not to be condemned, but on the contrary excused and tolerated.[260]

Luther claimed to reject the Roman Church in the same way as it (he alleged) had rejected both Scripture and the Church Fathers:

> But they would like to rule the church, not with trustworthy wisdom, but with arbitrary opinions, and again confuse and perplex all the souls in the world, as they have done before. But just as they reject all the Fathers and theologians in their petty canons, so do we, in turn, reject them in the church and in Scripture. They shall neither teach us Scripture nor rule in the church; they are not entitled to it, nor do they have the competence for it. But they shall attend to their trifling canons and squabbles over prebends—that is their holiness. They have cast us poor theologians, together with the Fathers, from their books; for this we thank them most kindly. Now they propose to throw us out of the church and out of Scripture; and they themselves are not worthy to be in them. That is

---

[259] Hendrix, 57,58.
[260] Ibid, 59.

too much, and rips the bag wide open. And furthermore, we shall not put up with it.²⁶¹

Luther's quotes were sometimes vehement reactions to the corruptions of the Church. This shows that reactions do not build proper teaching but may lead to total rejection of others' teachings. Such rejection includes the good part of the Catholic teaching that was Orthodox Patristic in its origin. In some other cases Luther did not maintain a balanced reaction, which led to a wider gap between him and the original Tradition.

Manfred Schulze in his analysis of Martin Luther and the Church Fathers raised the question of what makes the Church Fathers rank as Doctors of the church: He observes that Luther vehemently corrected the ancient Church and was not afraid to evaluate even the Fathers of the Church by their attitude towards the doctrine of justification. He quotes a preface, which was written in 1930: ²⁶²

> The article on justification by faith is the head and cornerstone which alone constitutes the church of God. Without this article it cannot exist for an hour [...] Therefore anyone who does not safeguard justification by faith cannot resist any of its opponents successfully.²⁶³

---

²⁶¹L W, Vol. 41, 162-163.

²⁶² Preface to *In Prophetam Amos Iohannis Brentii expositio* (1530), WA 30, 650, 17-33, cited in Schulze, M., *The reception of the Church Fathers in the West*, edited by Irena Backus, (Leiden: E.J. Brill, 1997), Vol. 2, 609-611.
²⁶³ Ibid, 611.

Consequently justification is very crucial as the main question of the Lutheran Reformation and Luther connected it with the acceptance of the so-called "Church Doctors". He puts it as a governing center that determines what is right and what is wrong. Schultze quotes Luther as follows:

> I have consequently been that more frequent amazed, almost indignantly, about what earned for Jerome the title of a *doctor Ecclesiae* and for Origen that of *Magister Ecclesiarum*... although it is hard to find three lines in them which teach the doctrine of justification, and although one cannot make anyone a Christian on the basis of any of their writings, as they come sweeping in so arrogantly with their allegories or allow themselves to be entrapped by the showiness of works. The same thing would have happened to Augustine if the Pelagians had not eventually exercised his full attention (*exercitium*) and driven him to the righteousness that is of faith. A *doctor Ecclesiae* is really the product of such a controversy and such practical experience *(exercitium)* and Augustine is almost the only one after the age of the Apostles and that of the earliest Church Fathers.[264]

In 1532, Luther states in *Table-Talk*-in the article "*Church Fathers Judged by the Gospel*"-that forgiveness of sins is the chief article in Christianity and through which one can judge the Fathers. In this article Luther raised Philip Melanchthon to be greater than Augustine. He declares that the Fathers who testify that the divine majesty pardons by grace, for the righteousness of men, are the true Fathers:

---

[264] Preface to In prophetam Amos Iohannis Brentii expositio (1530), WA 30^{II}, 650, 17-33 cited in ibid, 611.

Jerome can be read for the sake of history, but he has nothing at all to say about faith and the teaching of true religion. Origen I have already banned. I have no use for Chrysostom either, for he is only a gossip. Basil doesn't amount to anything; he was a monk after all, and I wouldn't give a penny for him. Philip's apology[265] is superior to all the doctors of the church, even to Augustine himself. Hilary and Theophylact[266] are good, and so is Ambrose.[267] The last sometimes treats excellently of the forgiveness of sins, which is the chief article, namely, that the divine majesty pardons by grace.[268]

It is obvious from the above quote his unbalanced stance towards the Fathers. He asserts on many occasions, as previously mentioned in this chapter, his honor in reading them and to learning from them what is scripturally approved, and then in the next breath he dismisses them all. What is even stranger in his behavior relates to St. Augustine. After he raised him to be the only one ranked "Doctor of the Church," he raised Melanchthon above him. Such an attitude reveals an unbalanced judgment inside Luther: implying that the gates of Hades prevailed against the Church for hundreds of years until he and his theologians appeared to reveal the lost truth.

---

[265] Melanchthon wrote *two* works: first the *Augsburg Confession* (1530) and then an *Apology of the Augsburg Confession* (1531). It's the second of these that Luther means.
[266] Theophylactos, archbishop of Achrida in the eleventh century.
[267] Ambrose, bishop of Milan (*ca.* 340–379), was a writer of ascetic and catechetical literature.
[268] L W, Vol. 54: *Table Talk*, 33-34.

Citing Hilary in *On the Trinity Book I*,[269] Luther notes that one should not use more or other words than those contained in Scripture.[270] However, later in contrast to this, he strongly recommends using new terms in the dialogues with the heretics and he accepted the term *homoousios* in the debate between Athanasius and Arius. He argues that similar terms are necessary to condense the meaning of Scripture, comprised of so many passages, into short and comprehensive words. Accordingly, the question will be summed up as to whether 'heretics' accept Christ as *homoousios* or not? He considered this term as the full meaning of all the words of Scripture that they had distorted with false interpretation. He applied the same rule in the debate with the Pelagians.[271]

Schulze emphasizes that Luther made the struggle against the Pelagians the central concern of any theology seeking to be called Christian. He sees Pelagianism as the constant threat to theology and the church. Moreover he affirms that the danger of Pelagian theology was much more prevalent in the days of Luther. So much so that the teachers of the Church at that time made grace something of very little worth and even a supplementary measure on the part of God[272]:

---

[269] Hilary of Poitiers, *On the Trinity*, in W. Sandy, eds. *The Nicene Fathers and Post-Nicene*, Series II, 9 v. (Edinburgh: T& T Clark, 1997), 18:50,51. In fact, according to Hilary, one should teach nothing that is at variance with Scripture.
[270] L W, Vol. 41, 83.
[271] Ibid, 83,84.
[272] Schulze, 579-585.

> Despite all progress in its theology, Luther affirmed that the church of his own day differed only terminologically but not in substance from the Pelagians: current established scholastic usage stated that we merit God's Grace even if not *de condigno*. But even Pelagians would have conceded this limitation.[273]

Schulze adds that Luther did not have the appropriate terminology and its historical development to differentiate between "nature" and "person" and he could not understand the concerns of Nestorius. He further said that Luther's starting point was that both Nestorius and Eutyches made Christ two persons. Meanwhile he stressed that Luther rightly grasped the elementary Christological problem of having to distinguish between the two natures, the divine and the human as opposed to the view that both are in one nature.[274] In general Schulze sees Luther learning from the faithful Councils' Fathers but he remained conservative, giving the highest authority to the Scriptures:

> Even if every quotation were appropriate and the fathers as authorities really did yield what they ought to yield, that would still not have produced of the legitimacy of theological statements. For above all the authorities of the fathers and of church decisions on doctrines stood *auctoritas* of Scripture:[275] "Even if Augustine and all the fathers were to see in Peter the Rock of the church, I will nevertheless oppose them- even as an isolated individual- supported by the authority of Paul and

---

[273] Ibid, 583.
[274] Ibid, 587.
[275] Ibid, 621.

therefore by divine law."[276]

This led Luther to find an answer to the question that raised itself, what are the purpose and the reason to hold a council. He summarizes the answer as follows:

> First, a council has no power to establish new articles of faith, even though the Holy Spirit is present. Even the apostolic council in Jerusalem introduced nothing new in matters of faith, but rather held that which St. Peter concludes in Acts 16 [15:11], and which all their predecessors believed, namely, the article that one is to be saved without the laws, solely through the grace of Christ. Second, a council has the power—and is also duty-bound to exercise it—to suppress and to condemn new articles of faith, in accordance with Scripture and the ancient faith, just as the Council of Nicaea condemned the new doctrine of Arius, that of Constantinople the new doctrine of Macedonius, that of Ephesus the new doctrine of Nestorius, and that of Chalcedon the new doctrine of Eutyches. Third, a council has no power to command new good works; it cannot do so, for Holy Scripture has already abundantly commanded all good works. What good works can one think of that the Holy Spirit does not teach in Scripture, such as humility, patience, gentleness, mercy, faithfulness, faith, kindness, peaceableness, obedience, self-discipline, chastity, generosity, readiness to serve, etc., and in summary, love? [Gal. 5:22–23]. What good work could one imagine that is not included in the commandment of love? What sort of a good work would it be if it were not motivated by love? For love, according to St. Paul's teaching, is the

---

[276] W A 59, 465, 1004-1006, cited in ibid, 621 (I could not trace it back).

fulfilment of the whole law [Gal. 5:14]—as Christ himself says in Matthew 5. Fourth, a council has the power—and is also duty-bound to exercise it—to condemn evil works that oppose love, according to all of Scripture and the ancient practice of the church, and to punish persons guilty of such works, as the Nicene council's decree rebuked the ambition and other vices of bishops and deacons. But here one should speak of two kinds of evil works: some that are, and are called clearly wicked, such as greed, murder, adultery, ambition, and the like. These we find condemned by the councils, as they are also condemned, outside the councils, in Holy Scripture and are, moreover, also punished by civil law. But besides these there are other, new good works which are not called evil, but are seemingly good, refined vices, holy idolatries invented by strange saints, or even mad saints; in summary, they are the white devil and a glittering Satan. Such evil, I should say new, good works should be condemned by the councils most sharply and severely, for they pose a danger to the Christian faith and an offence to Christian life and are a caricature or mockery of both.[277]

The first and second purposes mentioned above explain clearly what Luther meant by the external judgment of the ministry of the Word as stated in *On the Bondage of the Will* earlier in this chapter. Furthermore, it elucidates the role of the Church in matters of faith away from the internal judgment of the believer. However, the third and fourth purposes left no room for extra-scriptural teaching, and it omits all the apostolic practices which have no

---

[277] L W, Vol. 41, 123-124.

biblical warrants. Accordingly, Luther makes it hard for himself to keep the sacramental Tradition in his theology. This contradicts his early writings up to 1518, where he adopted sacramental theology. Additionally, Luther sees that Christ the Savior is exercised strongly in the sacramental signs of the church. Sacrament is the public act in which Christ bestows his grace in the life of the believer by faith. He disagreed with the Roman church over its sacramental theology. Even though none of the seven Councils made decrees on sacraments, his disagreement with the Roman Church in this point was a great stumbling block for Luther's theology.

Luther regarded the first four councils mentioned above, in which Chalcedon 451 was the last, as a clear sign that the aim of any faithful council is not to establish anything new but only to condemn the heretics' error against the old faith on the basis of Scripture. He argues in favor of these councils that they only preserved scriptural faith and defended it against the false interpretation. This confirms his view that no council headed by whosoever is allowed or authorized to think up a new articles concerning faith or good works. Thus, he criticized all other councils headed by Popes which established new articles of faith 'against the scriptures.' He asserts that the Fathers (the holy and good ones) cannot build without Scriptures that is gold, silver and precious stones and cannot mix it up with wood, straw or hay in the terms of St. Paul (I Cor. 3:12).[278] He remained very faithful in

---

[278] Ibid, 85,86.

defence of the superiority of scripture and as more reliable than all councils[279].

Luther attacked the majority of the Popes of the later councils because they set themselves up in Christ's stead as heads of the church and made the Holy Spirit subject to them. He avers that the Holy Spirit has no hand in their decretals and new establishments or articles of faith, but it was only the unholy spirit with his angels leading them. He called these new articles the 'white devil' and the 'glittering satan,' which should be condemned sharply by the faithful councils.[280] In actual fact he called them the devil's apostles, evangelists, and prophets, because the true apostles, evangelists, and prophets preach God's word, not against God's word.[281] Therefore, he stressed, the councils should condemn the heretic not according to their discretion, but rather according to the law of the empire, which is the Holy Scripture, confessed to be the law of the Holy Church.[282] He supplemented that by giving examples of real characters from the Scriptures, Balaam is a true prophet (Num24:16), and Judas is a true apostle (Matt 10:4) and the Pharisees occupying the seat of Moses to teach the truth (Matt.23:2-3). He then urged the need for 'something else' more reliable than the councils, and said this 'something else' is Holy

---

[279] Ibid, 119.
[280] Ibid, 124.
[281] Ibid, 155.
[282] Ibid, 133.

Scriptures.[283]

Luther added another proof from a booklet of Dr. "Pomer" (Bugenhagen) (1485-1528), *On the four chapters to the Corinthians*. He claims that he had learned from St. Augustine when he said he would believe none of the Fathers unless he has Scripture on his side.[284] Luther prayed "Dear God, if the Christian faith depended on men or was based on the words of men, what need would there be then for the Holy Scripture? Or why should God have given it? He respected the Fathers but he knows that all of them are human and they pray, "Forgive us our trespasses." He sees them not owning 'the promise of the Holy Spirit" that the apostles had but having 'the promise to be the apostles' disciples.'[285] Luther found a good partisan in Gregory of Nazianzen, the teacher of St. Jerome who lived in a better time and witnessed the glorious councils. He was amazed that they did not consider him a heretic although he attacked the councils severely when he says: [286]

> To tell the truth, I believe it advisable to flee all the councils of bishops; for I saw nothing good resulting from the councils, not even the abolition of evil, but rather sheer ambition and quarrelling over precedence," [287]

---

[283] Ibid, 120.
[284] Bugenhagen is referring to the same quotation from Augustine that used earlier in this chapter.
[285] Ibid, 49.
[286] Ibid, 119, 120.
[287] I could not check this saying, foot-noted in L W, Vol. 41 p 120 is: Epistola 130: ad Procopium. (MPG 37, 225–226).

Luther maintains that from the Fathers and the Councils we cannot collect all the teachings of the Christian faith. Scripture is the main source for Councils and Fathers, and without it the Church would not last long. He saw that the Church survived before the Councils and Fathers. Thus he has to speak differently about them seeking the meaning (spirit) not the letters.[288] He is astonished at the attempt of Gratian[289] to compare the discordant statements of Councils and Fathers, to reconcile the contradictions and to choose the best. Gratian succeeded in putting the best aside and chose the worst.[290]

Here I can see Luther missing something very important and very Orthodox as well. Scripture is seen at all times throughout the centuries as living by the saints and explained by the Fathers. From the Patristic writings of early Church, we can rewrite the whole New Testament except for a few verses. The Fathers were not separate from the Word. They lived it and explained it in an unbroken and harmonious way that which was identical to, and handed down from, Christ himself and the Apostles.

---

[288] L W Vol. 41, 52.
[289] The *Decretum* of Gratian, a Benedictine canonist at the law school of the University of Bologna. It originated in *ca.* 1140 and represents the first part of Roman Catholic canon law (*CIC* 1), accepted as such by Pope Gregory IX (1228–1241) in 1234, whose *Decretalium* became the second part of canon law (*CIC* 2). Luther studied it during his stay in Erfurt and in preparation for the Leipzig Debate in 1519.
[290] L W, Vol. 41, 20.

Council of Trent and Tradition

The Council of Trent (1545-1563), considered the nineteenth ecumenical council of the Roman Catholic Church, was the most important of the Sixteenth Century. Trent gave the definitive answer of the Roman Catholic Church to the Protestant claim for a thorough reformation of the Church. The Fourth Session (8th of February 1546 till 8th of April 1546) dealt with the matter of authority. The decree concerning Canonical Scriptures describes the "Gospel" as follows:

> [Having been] promised through the prophets in the Holy Scriptures, our Lord Jesus Christ, the Son of God, first promulgated [it] with His own mouth, and then commanded [it] to be preached by His Apostles to every creature, as the fountain of all, both saving truth, and moral discipline; and seeing clearly that this truth and discipline are contained in the written books, and the unwritten traditions which, received by the Apostles from the mouth of Christ himself, or from the Apostles themselves, the Holy Ghost dictating, have come down even unto us, transmitted as it were from hand to hand.[291]

This was a denial of the position known as *sola scriptura* whereby the Scripture alone possesses supreme authority in the Church. However, it did not finally commit the Roman Catholic Church to either a two source or a one-source theory of Revelation. Despite

---

[291] *The Council of Trent, the Fourth Session*, available [Internet] <http://history.hanover.edu/texts/trent/ct04.html> on [6th December 2004]

its reference to "unwritten traditions" it does not make it clear whether these traditions come directly from Christ and the Apostles without the medium of Scripture, or whether they have come orally from Christ (or the 'dictation' of the Holy Spirit) and have then been set down in written Scripture.

Tavard in his follow up on the council's sessions and statements before taking the decision on Scripture and Tradition, he sees a diversity of theologies. "One extreme is then neighbor to its opposite: the 'Scripture alone' of Schatzgeyer, the 'Church alone' of Prierias, or the 'continuing revelation' of Ellenbog."[292] Regarding the discussions of 27th of March he notes:

> At later stage in the discussions, Cornelio de Mussi, of Bitonto, will join the two ideas: a tradition concerning faith was intended by the Apostles themselves to be perpetually valid. Others were meant for a time only, while others still were matters of advice, never destined to be binding.[293]

The discussions did not make any distinctions between the three kinds of traditions mentioned above. While in the 23rd of March a group proposed a text aiming to separate between apostolic and non-apostolic traditions and to treat the former only in conjunction

---

[292] Tavard, 195.
[293] Ibid, 198.

with the Scripture.[294] However, this separation could not be achieved as well in the council sessions. Finally, Tavard concludes:

> Compared with pre-Tridentine theology, the decree of April 1546 makes it impossible to hold that new doctrines may still be revealed to the Church: the stress on apostolicity is too well marked to be compatible with such a view. It remains neutral on a notion of Tradition (in the singular), which would include Scripture and be identified with the life or conscience of the Church: the rationale of the Council precluded consideration of this problematic but did not gainsay the underlying theology. It finally respects the classical view: Scripture contains all revealed doctrine, and the Church's faith, which includes apostolic traditions, interprets it.[295]

In addition, the Latin Vulgate translation was declared the official biblical translation of the Church. In practice, if not in theory, this risked giving the Vulgate greater authority than the scriptural text in the source languages of Hebrew and Greek. For the first time the canon of Scripture was defined as including those deuterocanonical books that that the Protestant would eventually reject as canonical Scripture.[296]

Most importantly, however, Council of Trent also restated the Church's sole authority to interpret the Scriptures. Here we see a forerunner of the 19th century concept of the *Magisterium*, or

---

[294] Ibid, 199.
[295] Ibid, 208,209.
[296] *The Council of Trent, the Fourth Session*, available [Internet] http://history.hanover.edu/texts/trent/ct04.html> on [6th December 2004]

official teaching office of the Church.[297] The exclusive right of the Church to interpret Scripture was one of the positions that Luther had attacked in his tract *An Address to the Christian Nobility of the German Nation*[298]. Luther taught that the doctrine of the priesthood of believers meant that the individual Christian possessed the ability to interpret the Scriptures accurately. Although the Church did not officially denounce vernacular translations of the Bible, this canon effectively accomplished the same result.[299]

Conclusion

Luther started by rejecting the innovated doctrines that appeared in the Catholic Church after the Great Schism. The early Luther works (till 1518) can be considered as a an attempt to return to the Catholic Tradition which existed before the Great Schism. Luther's rejection of the human traditions remained till the end of his life.[300] Nevertheless, after Leo X's bull of November 1518, Luther found himself forced to fight against Rome:

> In that document, as Luther saw it, Leo arrogated to himself the power of defining the Church teaching without accountability to Scripture, the Fathers, or that ancient canons. This led Luther

---

[297] Ibid.
[298] Luther M., *An Address to the Christian Nobility of the German Nation*, available [Internet] <http://www.iclnet.org/pub/resources/text/wittenberg/luther/web/nblty-03.html> [6th December, 2004]
[299] Ibid
[300] Luther, *The Smalcald Articles, On Human Tradition*, Part III, Art. XV. Available [Internet] <http://www.iclnet.org/pub/resources/text/wittenberg/concord/web/smc-03o.html > [23rd March 2004]

eventually to conclude that the Roman Church was irrevocable committed to the claim that the authority of the pope stood even above Holy Scripture and it was in this context that he came, over the next several years, to believe that the papacy was the prophesied Antichrist of the last days, a conviction he then held to his dying day with a literalistic fever that his modern interpreters have rarely been willing to take as seriously as he did.[301]

Upon such stubbornness of the Church, Luther allocated all his energy to fight Church corruption. However, he changed his theological approach from being a reformer from within the Church, restoring the Catholic Tradition to its original Patristic form, to being a founder of another tradition according to his personal understanding of Scripture. In other words, Luther tried to take a balanced position with the Catholic Church in *Concerning Rebaptism* (1528) where he accepted many papal acts and rebuked the Anabaptist for saying "whatever of the Pope is Wrong" or "whatever is in the papacy we must have and do differently."[302] He was not so fanatical as to reject all what is under the papacy:

> The whole thing is nonsense. Christ himself came upon the errors of scribes and Pharisees among the Jewish people, but he did not on that account reject everything they had and thought (Matt. 23:3). We on our part confess that there is much that is Christian and good under the papacy;

---

[301] Yeago, David, "The Catholic Luther", *First Things: A Journal of Religion and Public life*, 61 (March 1996): 37-41. Also available [Internet] <http://www.firstthings.com/ftissues/ft9603/articles/yeago.html> [12th June 2003]

[302] L W, Vol. 40, 233.

indeed everything that is Christian and good is to be found there and has come to us from this source. For instance we confess that in the papal church there are the true holy Scriptures, true baptism, the true sacrament of the altar, the true keys to the forgiveness of sins, the true office of the ministry, the true catechism in the form of the Lord's Prayer, the Ten Commandments, and the articles of the creed. Similarly, the pope admits that we too, though condemned by him as heretics, and likewise all heretics, have the holy Scriptures, baptism, the keys, the catechism, etc. O how do you dissemble? How then do I dissemble? I speak of what the pope and we have in common. He on his part dissembles toward us and heretics and plainly admits what we and he have in common. I will continue to so dissemble, though it does me no good. I contend that in the papacy there is true Christianity, even the right kind of Christianity and many great and devoted saints. Shall I cease to make this pretence?[303]

Oberman sees in *Concerning Rebaptism* that Luther makes it very clear that his interpretation of *sola scriptura* principle does *not exclude, but includes* a high regard of Tradition I,[304] which was defined in Chapter II of this thesis. However, I can see this high regard of Tradition I as very selective. Luther ignores a lot of the cumulative interpretation of Scripture through history of the Church. His selections of the Fathers and their writings put Tradition I question and differ from the ideology of Tradition I of the late medieval understanding.

---

[303] L W, Vol. 40, 231-232.
[304] Oberman, *The Dawn of the Reformation*, 285.

Luther's adoption of *sola scriptura* closed the door in front of Tradition II, which also distanced him from the Orthodox Patristic understanding. This attitude encouraged him to deny most of the Church sacraments and in particular the Priesthood. Again such denial of the priesthood can be seen as a reaction to the corrupted priesthood of that time. Luther's dream for a council to determine the articles of faith is still desirable. It is very essential for the Orthodox Church to define the articles of faith that are needed for salvation in Tradition II, and to separate them from the cultural customs of local Churches. The Catholic Church requires the same determination. Such clear definitions will help in the ecumenical dialogues between any of the parties.

Other study shows that the Reformers 'deparentified' the Fathers. To "parentify a person" is to award authority and responsibility to that person which he or she neither earned nor deserved. By the same token, to "deparentify a person" is to refuse any longer to attribute inappropriate authority to that person and to assume more authority for oneself.[305] Schindler, the joint author of this study, concludes this concept of 'deparentification' and says:

> The appeal of Protestant reformers to the fathers was not, as have seen, uniform; on specific issues such as the presence of Christ they certainly disagreed. In general, however the reformers approached the fathers from a balanced stance which acknowledged both their limitations and their contributions, evangelical stance also

---

[305] Hendrix, 57.

remembered that the fathers were human beings as well as theological authorities. In an article written forty years ago Wilhelm Schneemelcher proposed, in specific reference to Athanasius, that similar attitude toward the fathers was appropriate for evangelical historians and theologians. The task of the patristic historian was not to condemn Athanasius as a politician or to glorify him as a saint, but to present him as a theologian, i.e. as a human being, who with all his deficits and mistakes struggled with perennial theology issues and who, with the means at his disposal, tried to realize the claim of God in his life. That attitude, it seems to me, was already anticipated by Protestant reformers in the sixteenth century.[306]

I can see Luther de-parentifying the Fathers. In many cases he was selective and rejected many of the Fathers teachings. The paradox here is that there were no limitations on such de-parentification. In his life, he degraded (to the extent of rejection) some writings of the New Testament like the epistle of James. He wrote on 1527 in lectures O*n the First Epistle of Peter*:

> But from this one can judge what true Christian doctrine or preaching is. For when one wants to preach the Gospel, one must treat only of the resurrection of Christ. He who does not preach this is no apostle. For this is the chief article of our faith. And those books that teach and stress this most are indeed the noblest books, as has been stated above.[5] This enables one to observe that the Epistle of James is no truly apostolic epistle, for it does not contain a single word about these things.[6] The greatest power of faith is bound

---

[306] Ibid, 68.

up in this article of faith. For if there were no resurrection, we would have no consolation or hope, and everything else Christ did and suffered would be futile (1 Cor. 15:17).[307]

Later in 1542, he attacked the epistle more vehemently:

> We should throw the Epistle of James out of this school; [308] for it doesn't amount to much. It contains not a syllable about Christ. Not once does it mention Christ, except at the beginning [Jas. 1:1; 2:1]. I maintain that some Jew wrote it who probably heard about Christian people but never encountered any. [309]

This shows that Luther re-canonized[310] the Scriptures known at his times. In other words, we find that he de-parentified the Fathers who canonized the Scripture (and the apostles, in a way) by his re-canonization. He doubts the authenticity of the writers of Scripture. This opened a door to other theologians, past, present and future, to reject and degrade any part of Scripture that did not suit their own teaching. This means he opened a door to lose the Scripture itself, as there were no limits to criticizing the Scriptures and the Scripture's writers as well.

Pelikan sympathizes with Luther (as the obedient rebel), or in Luther's words " By the grace of God, we are holy apostates." However, he states "The history of the Church has made the

---

[307] L W, Vol. 30, 12.
[308] He means the University of Wittenberg.
[309] L W, Vol. 54, 424.
[310] He did the same for the Old Testament, but it is not the place to discuss it here

formal anti-traditionalism of the Reformation obsolete"[311] and he adds "Examples from history of Orthodox, Protestant, and Roman Catholic theology, liturgy, piety, and polity support the thesis that, for better or for worse, or for a combination of the two Traditions are inevitable."[312] It is worth mentioning here that Prof. Pelikan himself converted to Orthodoxy on 25 March 1998. After he spent over fifty years of his life studying Tradition and issued five volumes on this subject. This was besides his work in editing the fifty-five volumes of Luther works plus about thirty other distinguished works.[313]

To sum it all up, Luther got caught in the dilemma of the four hundred years that preceded him. He found the Church of his days struggling with two sources of revelations. In some very basic doctrines, the contradictions with Scripture were very clear. He did not get the Orthodox Patristic understanding of the one source of revelation-which is Tradition. Even, if it were presented to him, the paradox from within Tradition II of his times would have forced him to reject it. Luther was fighting the corrupted innovated doctrines that claimed authority based in two sources of revelations. These two sources had many contradictions with the Church taking authority to endorse such contradictions. However, the one source of revelation of the Orthodox Patristic Church has

---

[311] Pelikan, 170.
[312] Ibid, 171.
[313] John Erickson, *Jaroslav Pelikan: The Living Legend in our Midst* Available [Internet] <http://www.svots.edu/Events/Summer-Institute/2003/readings/Pelikan-Legend.html> [24th March 2004].

extra-scriptural teachings with no such authority of the Church to accept or endorse any articles against the written Word of God.

5 ORTHODOX AND LUTHERAN IN DIALOGUE

In this chapter, I will investigate the roots of the ecumenical dialogues between the Lutheran and the Byzantine Orthodox family. The Oriental Orthodox family[314] has not started such a dialogue with the Lutheran Church yet. I will start with Melanchthon who is considered as one of the main Patristic theologians of the early Lutheran Reformation and a close friend of Luther. Melanchthon drafted some important confessional documents, notably the Greek version of the *Augsburg Confession*, which triggered the first dialogue between the Lutheran and the Orthodox Churches. Subsequently, I will explain the Orthodox understanding of the ecumenical dialogues, and finally followed by the history of these dialogues.

I will start with Jeremias II and the Tübingen theologians' correspondences and will show how fruitless these were at the end. Then, I will trace the dialogues that resulted from the constitution of the joint commission in 1981. I will also

---

[314] The Orthodox was divided into two families, the Byzantine and the Oriental since the fourth Ecumenical Council (451). Re-union document was signed in 1991 between both families but not effective yet.

highlight the plenaries that discussed Tradition and Scripture at the joint commission. Finally, in conclusion, I will highlight the paradox in understanding ecumenism between the Orthodox Church and the Lutherans and some of the achievements of these dialogues.

Melanchthon

Philip Melanchthon (1497-1560) is a German Reformer who has been often called "the quiet Reformer," the theologians' theologian, the methodical thinker and a literary genius.[315] He was born in Bretten, the son of George Schwarzerd. His uncle Johannes Reuchlin[316] gave him the Greek-derived name "Melanchthon" for his aptitude in languages and humanities. He graduated from Heidelberg, Tübingen and Wittenberg universities. He worked as a Professor of Greek at the University of Wittenberg upon the recommendation of Reuchlin (to elector Fredrick the Wise).[317]

Peter Fraenkel sums up the views of Melanchthon on the relation between the Scriptures and early Councils and says:

We can obtain an even clearer view of the relation

---

[315] Tibbs E., *16th Century Lutheran & Orthodox Exchange, Patriarch Jeremias II, The Tübingen Lutherans, and the Greek Version of the Augsburg Confession: A Sixteenth Century Encounter*, Fuller Theological Seminary, 2000. Available [Internet] <http://www.stpaulsirvine.org/html/lutherna.htm > [16th May, 2002]

[316] Reuchlin (1455-1522) German Humanist, Born in Pforzheim, he studied in Schlettstadt under the Brethren of the Common Life and attended in the University of Paris, see Douglas, 840-841.

[317] Douglas, 646-647.

between Scriptural and ecclesiastical authority if we return once more to the common places of 1521 and look at the curious argument about the early Councils and Scripture there. On the one hand exclusive concentration upon Scripture is recommended in so many words and is indeed the very purpose of the book: *Fallitur, quisquis aliunde christianismi formam petit quam e scriptura canonica.* Furthermore, the biblical principal is asserted against any attempts to impose as necessary anything that is merely human, as e.g. in the chapter *De Humanis Legibus*. Yet Melanchthon does not stop there. His problem is this: a Council as such has no guarantee that they will be led by the Spirit of truth.[318]

Melanchthon's ultimate standard of judgment in all questions including the authority of the church and the Holy writ is the *"fundamentum."* He derived this term from I Cor. 3:11-15 and sometimes he combined it with Eph. 2:20. Fraenkel sees this *"fundamentum"* as problematic because it leaves three types of interpretations. First as some historians see in this foundation a limited conception of doctrine which can be compared with the *"articuli fundamentales"* of the Lutherans—which enables them to have the double role of an ultimate standard of doctrine and universal minimum orthodoxy. Second is that others suggest that Melanchthon makes use of many definitions and expressions which look paradoxical or at least vague. These cover issues such as the person of Christ through the Scriptures and the Articles of Faith. Additionally he restates the Creeds to conform to this 'foundation'.

---

[318]Peter Fraenkel, *Testimonia Patrum, The Function of The Patristic Argument In The Theology Of Philip Melanchthon*, (Geneve :Librairie E. Dros, 1961), 34-35.

Third is that Hoffmann[319] shows that Melanchthon uses insufficient and incompatible terminology which makes it difficult to find a common formula for his definitions. Fraenkel adds that these three interpretations make it impossible to escape from concluding that his exegesis is problematic, and reflects Melanchthon's own uncertainty.[320] In defining the relation between this 'foundation' and the Holy writ Fraenkel says:

> To put last things first, we should note that when Melanchthon speaks of the absolute standard of judgment for the Fathers, or the rule according to which their theology should be critically expurgated and completed, he tends to equate the Scriptures and the *Fundamentum*..... But as we have seen the very possibility of such an expurgation presupposes that the critic and the Church Fathers are, in absolute terms, both within the Church. This means that they share the foundation, which is not only intellectual yard-stick of true doctrine, but also at the same time their common doctrinal presupposition, the source and basis of their faith. We have also seen Melanchthon argue that the exclusive, absolute authority and aspect of the faith, but that if the scriptural test is accepted and passed, conciliar decisions can become articles of faith. This goes hand in hand with the idea that only truly patristic theology is scriptural, since the Fathers themselves confessed the Scriptures to be the ultimate presupposition, source and axiom of their teaching.[321]

Meijering, in his analysis of Melanchthon's Patristic

---

[319] Hoffman, *Fides Implicata*, Vol 2, 151 quoted in ibid, 338.
[320] Ibid, 338,339.
[321] Ibid, 342, 343.

thought, notes that he used the Fathers to define the relation between ecclesiastic Tradition and Scripture in opposition to the authority of the Pope. Melanchthon quotes Ambrose, Augustine, Basil Chrysostom, Cyprian, Hilary of Poitiers, Irenaeus, Jerome, Origen and Tertullian. Meijering sums up Melanchthon desposition to the Fathers:

> According to Melanchthon the theology of the Fathers is fairly close to Scriptural revelation, not as close as Melanchthon himself claims to be, but certainly much closer than the Scholastic. This also becomes apparent, according to Melanchthon, in their attitude towards the Bible. They want to use Scriptures as the exclusive norm of their theology, but do not follow this intention consistently, since they also come forward with new traditions which are incompatible with revelation given in Scripture.[322]

Melanchthon asserts that there is no guarantee for a council to be led by the Spirit of Truth. However, this statement makes the church live in uncertainty and it shows that Christ may desert his Church to the gates of hell to prevail against it. Of course, not every council or decree is made under the guidance of the Holy Spirit, but there are a lot of Councils and decrees which were led and guided by the Holy Spirit. This leaves the issue which council or decree is true. This leads to the One Holy Tradition as the true guard for the 'Catholic Truth' throughout the history of the

---

[322] E. Meijering, *Melanchthon And Patristic Thought, The Doctrine OF Christ and Grace, The Trinity And The Creation*, (Leiden: E.J Brill, 1983), 93.

Church.

According to Fraenkel, Melanchthon is trying to steer a middle way between (1) Anabaptists who believe that tradition is completely *unnecessary* and (2) some Catholics who try to argue that Church and Tradition have a *higher* authority than that of Scripture. According to Fraenkel[323] Melanchthon believes that Tradition embodied in Fathers, councils etc. and *is* necessary for Christians today, but it is also subordinate to Scripture. Melanchthon doesn't believe that there is an apostolic succession of bishops, but he *does* believe that there is an historical succession of teachers/preachers (*successio doctorum*), such as the fathers, who bear witness (*testimonium*) in each generation to what scriptural teaching (the *fundamentum*) is. For Melanchthon Tradition shows us now that this *fundamentum* has remained unchanged since the time of the apostles—even though, sometimes, only a small number of Christians held on to it, and the rest fell into heresy. So the Fathers are like witnesses in a court.[324] If there weren't witnesses, the judge and jury couldn't know what happened. True witnesses testify to the truth (i.e. of Scripture), but they can't change it unless they become false witnesses. So— for Melanchthon— Christ is always with his church, through the work of the Spirit, who guides a succession of teachers/preachers in bearing witness to the truth written in Scripture. In fact, the doctrine of Scripture couldn't be passed on to us without them. However, because they're always human, their teaching has always

---

[323] Fraenkel, 61, 186, 152f, 225.
[324] Ibid, 225-235.

to be tested against Scripture to ensure that they are teaching under the guidance of the Holy Spirit. To put it another way: the Scripture is never without a Ministry of the Word and the Ministry of the Word is never without Scripture. This is a kind of Protestant version of Oberman's Tradition I: i.e., a tradition/*paradosis* that comes from Scripture alone, but is utterly necessary if the message of Scripture is to be explained and taught.

It is worth mentioning here that this is highly consistent with the quotation regarding Tradition I from Oberman in Chapter 2 page 30, 31.

Fraenkel and Meijering note and confirm the uncertainty of Melanchthon's exclusive use of the Bible. Fraenkel sees Melanchthon contradicting his 'foundation'. While Meijering did show that Melanchthon came with new traditions, which were incompatible with Scripture, he did not give examples of such traditions. In other words, both of them see inconsistency in his way of treating Scripture and Tradition.

Meijering concludes that Melanchthon wanted to be an anti-speculative theologian who based his doctrine first and foremost on Scripture and in the second position on the Fathers. He sees variance between the late Melanchthon and the young one, but he describes it as development rather than a break or contradiction. As a young Reformer Melanchthon never changed his focus on salvation by grace alone. The development was that he moved from dwelling on this exclusively to, in his later years, setting it in a wider context. According to Meijering there is yet another contradictory position, as Melanchthon once claimed to believe in the consensus of the Fathers in certain subjects and in other occasions he picked up from the Fathers what seemed attractive to him. Additionally, he often gives the impression that he presents the consensus of the Father and rarely does he admit the opposite[325]. Meijering describes the influence of the Father on Melanchthon and says:

> If one asks whether the Fathers really influenced Melanchthon or whether he used the Fathers as supporters of views which he already held, there can be little doubt that the latter was the case. He had a number of quotations from the Fathers in store which he had either found himself in their writings or to which contemporaries drew his attention, and he used these quotations wherever it suited him, and he merely ignored what did not suit him. Not seldom he –consciously or unconsciously- twisted his quotations in such a way that they suited him even more. When in the course of his life there was a development in his thought on various matters, he obviously looked for more and other quotations from the Fathers which could support his views.[326]

Melanchthon's background knowledge of the Fathers, and thoughts as described above by Fraenkel and Meijering, enabled him to drew up many important works such as the *Visitation Articles* (1528), the *Augsburg Confession* (1530), the *Apology of the Augsburg*

---

[325] Ibid, 138,139.
[326] Ibid, 139.

Confession (1531), the *Confessio Saxonica* (1551), and he formulated the *Wittenberg Concord* (1536).[327] The *Augsburg Confession* was written upon the proclamation of a Diet in Augsburg by Charles V on 21st January 1530, and read on 25th June 1530. It is considered the most important. Schaff describes the formation of it:

> If we look at the contents, Luther is the primary, Melanchthon the secondary, author; but the form; the method, style, and temper are altogether Melanchthon's. Nobody else could produce such a work. Luther would have made it more aggressive and polemic, but less effective for the occasion. He himself was conscious of the superior qualification of his friend for the task, and expressed his entire satisfaction with the execution. "It pleases me very well," he wrote of the Confession, "and I could not change or improve it; nor would it be becoming to do so, since I cannot tread so softly and gently." He would have made the tenth article on the real presence still stronger than it is; would have inserted his *sola* in the doctrine of justification by faith, as he did in his German Bible; and rejected purgatory, and the tyranny of popery, among the abuses in the second part. He would have changed the whole tone, and made the document a trumpet of war.[328]

In 1530 the Latin version of the confession appeared, on which the Greek version of the confession *Augustana Graeca* was based and described by Florovsky as "a document of very peculiar

---

[327]Douglas, 647.
[328] Schaff, Vol.7, 532.

character."[329] The Greek version which appeared on 1559 was not a translation but a re-working of the whole text in the interest of building bridges between the East and West. Tibbs confirms that it has been edited under the name of Paul Dolscius, but composed by Philip Melanchthon. He asserts that the nuances of the text were neither serving as a camouflage, as Jorgensen put it, nor was it just a translation as the author of it states at its beginning[330]. Tibbes sees, with Korte, in *Augustana Graeca* a need for changes of the terminology to remove theological obstacles. Additionally, Korte the Lutheran theologian, believes that such adaptation in language to suit the reader was not satisfactory but compulsory in light of his aim of minimizing the gap between the Greeks and Reformers:

> In all justice to the translator of the Augsburg Confession into Greek, we must see the great difficulties he encountered. These involved differences in language and piety. The Latin language was formed by the Roman mind, its laws and its institution, and these Roman conceptions were transferred to the religious realm.[331]

The Orthodox Lutheran dialogue

Before we start to investigate the Orthodox-Lutheran Dialogues, it is important to consider the Orthodox understanding of the meaning and aim of ecumenical dialogues as presented in the third

---

[329] George Florovsky, *Collected Works of Georges Florovsky, Vol. II, Christianity and Culture*, (Belmont MA: Norland publishing, 1974), 148.
[330] Tibbs, 11-12.
[331] Korte B., "Early Lutheran Relations with Eastern Orthodox", *The Lutheran Quarterly*, Vol. IX number I, (February 1957), cited in Tibbs, 13.

Assembly of the World Council of Churches in New Delhi in 1961:

> In this situation the Orthodox Representatives feel themselves obliged to underline the basic difference between their own approach to the ecumenical problem and that which is implied in the document of St Andrews. The ecumenical problem, as it is understood in the current ecumenical movement, is primarily a problem of the Protestant world. The main question, in this setting, is that of "Denominationalism". Accordingly, the problem of Christian unity, or of Christian Reunion, is usually regarded in terms of an interdenominational agreement or Reconciliation. In the Protestant universe of discourse such approach is quite natural. But for the Orthodox it is uncongenial. For the Orthodox the basic ecumenical problem is that of schism. The Orthodox cannot accept the idea of a "parity of denomination" and cannot visualize Christian Reunion just as an interdenominational adjustment. The unity has been broken and must be recovered. The Orthodox Church is not a confession, one of many, one among the many. For the Orthodox, the Orthodox Church is just the Church. The Orthodox Church is aware and conscious of the identity of her inner structure and of her teaching with the Apostolic message (kerygma) and the tradition of the ancient undivided Church. She finds herself in an unbroken and continuous succession of sacramental ministry, sacramental life, and faith. Indeed, for the Orthodox the apostolic succession of episcopacy and sacramental priesthood is an essential and constitutive, and therefore obligatory element of the Church's very existence. The Orthodox Church, by her inner conviction and consciousness, has a special and exceptional position in the divided Christendom, as the bearer

of, and the witness to, the tradition of the ancient undivided Church, from which all existing denominations stem, by the way of reduction and separation. From the Orthodox point of view, the current ecumenical endeavor can be characterized as "ecumenism in space", aiming at agreement between various denominations, as they exist at present. This endeavor is, from the Orthodox point of view, quite inadequate and incomplete.

The common ground, or rather the common background of existing denominations, can be found, and must be sought, in the past in their common history, in that common ancient and apostolic tradition, from which all of them derive their existence. This kind of ecumenical endeavor can be properly denoted as "ecumenism in time". The report of Faith and Order itself mentions "agreement (in faith) with all ages" as one of the normative prerequisites of unity. Orthodox theologians suggest this new method of ecumenical inquiry, and this new criterion of ecumenical evaluation, as a kingly rock, with the hope that unity may be recovered by the divided denominations by their return to their common past. By this way divergent denominations may meet each other on the unity of common tradition. The Orthodox Church is willing to participate in this common work as the witness which had preserved continuously the deposit of apostolic faith and tradition. No static restoration of old forms is anticipated, but rather a dynamic recovery of perennial ethos, which only can secure the true agreement "of all ages". Nor should there be a rigid uniformity, since the same faith, mysterious in its essence and unfathomable adequately in the formulas of human reason, can be expressed accurately in different manners. The immediate objective of the ecumenical search is, according to the Orthodox understanding, a reintegration of Christian mind, a recovery of apostolic tradition, a fullness of Christian vision and belief, in agreement with all ages.[332]

Based on the above mentioned Orthodox understanding of ecumenism and dialogues, the history of such attempts and its results are considered. Florovsky sees that the initiation of the relations was as early as 1557, he says:

> In 1557 a special Swedish delegation visited Moscow. Two prominent Church leaders were among the delegates – Laurentius Perti, the first Lutheran Archbishop of Uppsala, and Michael Agricola, the Finnish Reformer. The delegates met with the Metropolitan of Moscow (Macarius), obviously on the initiative of the Tsar Ivan the Terrible. The main topics for discussion were the veneration of icons and fasting. Greek was the language of the conversation, but Russian interpreters were very poor. The episode is interesting as a proof of interest on both sides in the religious aspect of relationship between the two nations. [333]

In 1558-1559 Patriarch Joasaph II (1555-65) of Constantinople sent Serbian Deacon Demetrios Mysos to Wittenberg to collect information about the doctrines and way of life of the Reformers. There he met Melanchthon and worked out with him the Greek version of *Augsburg confession*. On its completion, it was sent via this

---

[332] G. Patelos, *The Orthodox Church in the Ecumenical Movement, Documents and Statement*, 1902-1975, (Geneva: World Council of Churches, 1978), 97-98.
[333] George Florovsky, *The Orthodox Church and The Ecumenical Movement Prior to 1910*, in *A History Of The Ecumenitcal Movement*, eds. by Ruth Rouse and Stephen Charles Neil, *Vol.1*, (London: SPCK, 1986), 177.

deacon to the Patriarch on 1558. However, there are claims that the deacon was killed in a rebellion in Wallachia and the letter of Melanchthon and the first copy of the translation never arrived at Constantinople and as a result the communication stopped for a while.[334]

Later, in October, 1573 Baron David Ungnad von Sonnegk, the new imperial ambassador to Turkey was appointed. He was a devout Lutheran and studied law in Tübingen[335]. He made a visit to Constantinople with his Lutheran chaplain Stephen Gerlach who carried with him an introductory letter from Jakob Andreae[336]. Correspondences took place during 1574-1582. In May 24, 1575 Gerlach personally presented to the Patriarch the *Augustana Graeca*, which was entitled by the Lutheran "*A Confession of the Orthodox Faith.*"[337]

The Patriarch of Constantinople at that time was Jeremias II who was only 36 years old when he was elected the 173rd successor of the first founder of the Church in Constantinople, the Apostle Andrew, and the 19th ecumenical patriarch after the fall of Byzantium (1453). He was from a righteous family highly regarded for its devoutness and high social rank and influence. He surrounded himself with highly educated

---

[334] Tibbs, 14.
[335] Ibid, 15.
[336] Jakob Andreae (1528 -1590) Lutheran theologian born in Waiblingen, he was the most famous theologian of his time, he worked unceasingly for unity and to purify in Lutheran doctrine, see Dougals, 40.
[337] Florovsky, *Christianity and Culture*, 145.

men who were steeped in Greek and Latin thought and was the first to establish a publishing house in Constantinople. Tibbs quotes Runciman as follows: "Jeremias II was probably the ablest man to sit on the Patriarch throne during the captivity. He was a sound theologian, an ardent reformer and a fierce enemy to simony."[338]

The correspondences started in a very good atmosphere, full of love, which was very clear in the language used. For Example, the Lutherans addressed Jeremias II with such terms as: "Most Honourable Lord," "All Holy Sir," "Most God-beloved Sir," and "Your Holiness." Certainly, this is totally opposite to their addresses to the Catholic bishops who have been described by Melanchthon as "the asses upon which they ride." In the same way Jeremias II replied calling them: "Most wise Germans" and his Spiritual sons. However, Jeremias II asserts that no religious leader can innovate, raise contradictions or additions to the Holy Traditions of the Church throughout her existence.[339]

Tibbs sees that Jeremias II was obliged to end the dialogue in his third reply. He believed it was necessary to respond only according to the consensus of Patristic thought, and the Tübingen theologians were clearly rejecting any source as authoritative other than Scripture. He quotes Jeremias:

Therefore we request that from henceforth you do

---
[338] Tibbs, 7.
[339] Ibid, 16-18.

> not cause us more grief, nor write to us on the same subject if you should wish to treat these luminaries and theologians of the Church in a different manner. You honour and exalt them in words, but you reject them in deeds. For you try to prove our weapons which are their holy and divine discourses as unsuitable. And it is with this document that we would have to write and contradict you. Thus, as for you, please release us from these cares. Therefore, going about your own ways, write no longer concerning dogmas; but if you do, write only for friendships sake. Farewell.[340]

Nevertheless, they replied in a gracious and friendly way:

> And even if you ask us to no longer trouble you with such writings (although we have conversed with much love and much kindness and with due respect) yet we are hopeful that the matters which have been written to you by us up to now will in time be re-examined and reconsidered more accurately and much better ... Therefore, standing together with your Holiness, Patriarch and Most Reverend Sir, we offer to the God of all, our true friendship which we have shown to you and which we continuously afterwards keep.[341]

Florovsky sums up the whole period of correspondences and says:

> The reply of the Patriarch Jeremias II was friendly, but disappointing from the Lutheran point of view. The Patriarch suggested that the Lutherans should join the Orthodox Church and accept its traditional teaching. He wrote in his own name, as an individual and not with synodical authority, but

---

[340] Ibid, 19.
[341] Ibid, 20.

naturally he had the advice and co-operation of other Greek hierarchs and scholars. It seems that Theodosius Zygomalas was the main contributor, but the final draft was carefully revised by Jeremias himself. The document was by no means an original composition, nor did it claim originality. It was deliberately complied from traditional sources. The main authorites were Nicolas Cabasilas, Symeon of Thessalonica, and Joseph Brynnios, all renowned Byzantine theologians of the 14th and 15th centuries, and among the early Fathers, especially St. Basil and St. John Chrysostom. Great emphasis was laid on loyalty to tradition. This constituted the greatest difficulty for the Lutherans, with their emphasis on 'Scripture only'.[342]

Tibbs presents the summarized conclusions of Jorgensen, where he states the points of doctrinal agreements and of disagreements. Holy Tradition was at the top of the list of disagreement points, in addition to the infallibility of the Church; the Ecumenical councils; the veneration, feasts and invocation of saints and their icons and relics, as well as fasts and other ecclesiastical traditions and customs. Although it is clear that no agreement had been achieved, it was a good start in getting to know each other and to put clearly the points of convergence and divergence in their place.[343] After this dialogue the Eastern Church grew weaker in its political influence and came under more severe persecutions by the Islamic invaders. However, Florovsky notes with surety:

---

[342] Florovsky, The *Orthodox Churches and The Ecumenical Movement Prior to 1910*, 178.
[343] Ibid, 21-22.

> But Byzantium is still alive in the things of the spirit, the representative of an authentic Christian Tradition, linked by unbroken continuity with the thought of the apostolic age. Recovery of a genuine ecumenical unity will be possible only through mutual rediscovery of East and West and a wider synthesis, such as has sometimes been attempted but never yet achieved.[344]

After that, Constantinople received overtures from both Catholics and Protestant. These contacts reached their climax when Cyril Lukaris[345] (1572-1638) became Patriarch. His experiences of Jesuit propaganda in Poland and Lithuania influenced his attitude and necessitated the help of Protestants in defending against Latin aggression[346] His *Confession of Faith* was printed in Geneva on 1629. This confession leads most historians such as Gibbon to call him "the Protestant Patriarch."[347] It was a Calvinist document by any standard where Hadjiantoniou describes:

> This thoroughly Calvinist document taught that the Church was subject to Scripture and could err; predestination to eternal life irrespective of good works; justification by faith; two sacraments; and a Reformed doctrine of the Eucharist. This statement caused a reaction in Europe. The confession's effect upon Orthodox Church was limited, however, since it was repudiated shortly

---

[344] Florovsky, *Christianity and Culture*, 162.
[345] He knew much about the Western Ways, for he studies in Venice, Padua, he became the Patriarch of Alexandria in 160, and Patriarch of Constantinople in 1612, see Douglas, 607.
[346] Nicolas Zernov, *Eastern Christendom: A Study of the Origin and Developments of the Eastern Orthodox Church*, (London: Weildenfeld and Nicolson, 1961), 137.
[347] Gibbon E., *The History of The Decline and Fall of The Roman Empire*, Vol. 4, (USA: Albany, 1997), 689.

after Cyril's death. Finally in 1672 the Great Orthodox Synod of Jerusalem formally condemned the "error" of Protestantism.[348]

It is obvious that this first attempt of contact between Orthodox and Lutherans highlighted clearly that the key issue was the Holy Tradition. Most, if not all, points of disagreement related to the Lutheran understanding of Tradition in terms of two sources of revelations in contradiction to the one source of the Orthodox. This identified the problem very early. However, the deep discussions of the sources of revelation took place four centuries later.

Since then the dialogue has nearly stopped. Both churches were distant from each other, mainly for political reasons and internal sufferings. In the twentieth century the dialogue resumed when high-level visits between the Ecumenical Patriarchate and the Lutheran World of Federation (LWF), and separate deliberations on both sides, began in 1967. The Fourth Pan-Orthodox Conference officially encouraged a global ecumenical dialogue with the LWF as early as 1968. That same year the LWF Executive Committee discussed and approved plans for participation in such a dialogue. A thorough preparatory process led to decisions by the Orthodox in 1976 and by the Lutherans in 1977 to further develop and implement plans for dialogue by means of separate Orthodox and Lutheran meetings, which took place in 1978, 1979 and 1980.

---

[348] Douglas, 607.

The Lutheran-Orthodox Joint Commission met for the first time in Espoo, Finland in 1981.[349]

The Joint commission issued eight statements, the first one was on *Divine Revelation* (3rd Plenary, Allentown 1985), second on *Scripture and Tradition* (4rd, Crete 1987), third on *The Canon and the Inspiration of the Holy Scripture* (5th, Bad Segeberg 1989). While the following three statements were titled *Authority in and Of the Church*, with the subtitles *The Ecumenical Councils* (7th, Sandbjerg 1993), *Understanding of Salvation in the Light of the Ecumenical Councils* (8th, Limassol 1995), *Salvation: Grace, Justification and Synergy* (9th, Sigtuna 1998). Two further statements titled *The Mystery of the Church*, with subtitles *Word and Sacraments (Mysteria) in the Life of the Church* (10th, Damascus 2000), and *Mysteria/ Sacraments as Means of Salvation* (11th, Oslo 2002) were issued.[350]

The third plenary asserts in the fourth article that the Holy Spirit sustains the church's life and growth until the last day through the proclamation of the gospel in the fullness of the apostolic Tradition and its transmission from place to place. Such transmission is not only by words but also by the whole life of the Church. Additionally, it confirms in the fifth article that under the guidance of the Holy Spirit, divine revelation is living in the church

---

[349] *The official web site of LWF.* Available [Internet] <http://www.lutheranworld.org/What_We_Do/OEA/Bilateral_Relations/OEA-Lutheran-Orthodox.html> [20th December 2003]
[350] *Lutheran- Orthodox Joint commission.* Available [Internet] <http://www.helsinki.fi/~risaarin/lutortjointtext.html> [20th December 2003]

through Holy Scripture and Holy Tradition. Finally in the sixth article they quote St. Athanasius:

> The sacred and divinely inspired scriptures are sufficient for the exposition of the truth, but there also exist many treatises of our blessed teachers composed for this purpose, and if one reads them he will gain somehow the right interpretation of the scriptures.[351]

The plenary here in quoting St. Athanasius puts emphasis on Tradition I. However, the term used by St. Athanasius "our blessed teachers" is obscured for Lutherans. For Lutherans, the status teacher or Father is always debatable and it does not have the same weight as for the Orthodox. A clearer definition of a Church teacher or Father is needed to facilitate points of agreements in further discussions.

The fourth plenary focused more on the relation between Scripture and Tradition, where it states (second and third articles) that Tradition is the authenticated tool to transfer the *"euangelion"* of Jesus Christ through the work of the Holy Spirit to the living church to the end of the ages. Articles four, six and seven stress that the *"euangelion"* of salvation is the content of holy Tradition, preserved, confessed and transmitted in scripture, in the lives of the saints in all ages, and in the conciliar tradition of the church. Since Holy Scripture is the work of the Holy Spirit in Holy Tradition, it works as the criterion for true understanding of Jesus

---

[351] St. Athanasius, *Oratio Contra Gentes, 1*, 3, PG 25,4 cited in ibid.

Christ himself in the life and teaching of the one, holy, catholic and apostolic church. This, however, is conditioned by the catholic experience of salvation in the church is at the same time the only authentic expression of the true understanding of the word of God.[352]

Articles eight, nine and ten agree on the authority of the Fathers, councils, and church decisions, although they comment on which teaching should be considered as Orthodox. Moreover, they see the function of Holy Scripture is to serve the authenticity of the church's living experience in safeguarding the holy Tradition from all attempts to falsify the true faith, not to undermine the authority of the church, the body of Christ. Article eight explains:

> The holy Tradition as the ongoing action of the Holy Spirit in the Church expresses itself in the church's whole life. The decisions of the ecumenical councils and local synods of the church, the teaching of the holy fathers and liturgical texts and rites are especially important and authoritative expressions of this manifold action of the Holy Spirit. However, not every synod claiming to be orthodox, not every teaching of an ecclesiastical writer, not all rites are expressions of the holy Tradition, if they are not accepted by the whole church. They may be only human traditions, lacking the presence of the Holy Spirit. That is why the problem of the criteria for determination of the presence of the holy

---

[352] Ibid.

Tradition in the traditions of the churches is of great importance and needs further study.[353]

This article is very important in pointing to the real problem, which is the needed determination from the Orthodox side as to what it is in the Holy Tradition that is essential for salvation. However, this will not stop the Orthodox from keeping their local customs, which are not in contradiction with Scripture but still without biblical warrant. Additionally, the Orthodox need a list of points of agreement and disagreement from the Lutherans about the decrees of the seven accepted Councils. Such a list will help in developing the acceptance and determination of councils and synods, whether in the past or in the future.

Articles eleven and twelve agree that pointing to Scripture are pointing to the "*euangelion*" of salvation, to Christ and therefore to the holy Tradition, which is the life of the church. Scripture acts as the criterion of its authenticity and stresses the church's unity and catholicity for the joyful common praise of the triune God. Additionally, the Orthodox Church accepted the meaning intended by *sola scriptura* as it explains in article eleven:

> Regarding the relation of scripture and Tradition, for centuries there seemed to have been a deep difference between Orthodox and Lutheran teaching. Orthodox hear with satisfaction the affirmation of the Lutheran theologians that the formula *sola scriptura* was always intended to point

---
[353] Ibid.

to God's revelation, God's saving act through Christ in the power of the Holy Spirit, and therefore to the Holy Tradition of the Church, as expressed in this paper, against human traditions that darken the authentic teaching in the church.[354]

Apparently the wording of this article is a great step towards a mutual understanding. In other words, the Orthodox recognized that the Lutheran formulation *sola scriptura* need not be inconsistent with their emphasis on the primacy of Tradition. Additionally, the article points to some work to be done by both sides to determine the human traditions.

In the fifth plenary article three declares that the parts of Tradition regarding the incarnate Lord himself and the message of the apostles were joined to the Holy Scriptures of Israel as their fulfillment and completion (Heb. 10:11; 2 Cor. 3: 3-18). These new writings, a deposit of the apostolic oral Tradition, became the New Testament. Additionally in article five they consider the recognition of the Holy Scriptures of the Old and New Testaments, the Christian Bible, is one of the most important decisions of the Church on its way from Pentecost to the last judgment. They believe and teach together that the Church was led by the Holy Spirit in this decision. The two churches have consensus about the content of the New Testament.[355] The agreement on the content of the New Testament went some way towards settling the potential

---

[354] Ibid.
[355] Ibid.

difficulties raised by Luther's doubts about some of its books that were discussed in the previous chapter.

Article twelve addresses the inspiration of the books of the Holy Scripture and points back to the working of the Spirit in their production, that is to say, the inspiration of the authors, and points forward to the working of this same Spirit in the church who teaches how the Scriptures are to be understood and leads the faithful to their goal. Article thirteen starts: "According to the apostolic witnesses and the teaching of the Fathers" to emphasize the continuity of teaching from the apostolic era to date. The interpretation of the Scriptures is continued in the life of the church as elucidated in article seventeen:

> The interpretation of revelation and inspiration consummated in Pentecost continues in the life of the church. Within the life of the church Christians who become "a temple of the Holy Spirit" (1 Corin. 6:19) and therefore are members of the body of Christ are led into all the truth in the experience of glorification, as the Lord prayed to the Father: "Father, I desire that they also, whom thou hast given me, may be with me where I am, to behold my glory which thou hast given me in thy love for me before the foundation of the world" (John 17:24).[356]

The last article in this fifth plenary, article nineteen, defines who can interpret the Scriptures and in what capacity from both points of views; the Orthodox and the Lutherans:

---
[356] Ibid.

> Authentic interpreters of the Holy Scripture are persons who have had the same experience of revelation and inspiration within the body of Christ as the biblical writers had. Therefore it is necessary for authentic understanding that anybody who reads or hears the Bible be inspired by the Holy Spirit. The Orthodox believes that such authentic interpretation is the service of the Fathers of the church especially expressed in the decisions of the ecumenical councils. Lutherans agree in principle. Lutheran confessional writings affirm that no one can believe in Jesus Christ by one's own reason or abilities but that it is the Holy Spirit who calls, gathers and illuminates believers through the gospel even as he calls, gathers and enlightens the whole church on earth keeping it in union with Jesus Christ in the one true faith (Luther's Small Catechism).[357]

The seventh plenary discusses the authority *in* and *of* the Church, in particular the ecumenical councils. It asserts, in the first article, that the Church's authority is based on God's saving revelation in Jesus Christ to which the Scriptures of the Old and New Testaments and Holy Tradition bear witness. The second article explains that such authority is originated in the saving works of Christ, thus authority and soteriology are inseparable and present at all times in the Church's mission through the work of the Holy Spirit. Accordingly this plenary agreed that the ecumenical councils are a special gift of God to the church to preserve and transmit the faith once delivered to the saints. The third article is a consensus on the seven ecumenical councils and their decisions:

---

[357] Ibid.

> The seven ecumenical councils of the early Church were assemblies of the bishops of the Church from all parts of the Roman Empire to clarify and express the apostolic faith. These councils are Nicaea (325 A.D.), Constantinople I (381), Ephesus (431), Chalcedon (451), Constantinople II (553), Constantinople III (680/81), and Nicaea II (787). Of the councils it was stated at Crete in 1987: "The Holy Tradition as ongoing action of the Holy Spirit in the Church expresses itself in the Church's whole life. The decisions of the ecumenical councils and local synods of the Church, the teaching of the holy Fathers and liturgical texts and rites are especially important and authoritative expressions of this manifold action of the Holy Spirit" (par. 8). Ecumenical councils are the epitome of biblical theology and they summarize main themes of the Holy Tradition. They are not merely of historical significance but are irreplaceable events for the Church's life. Through them the apostolic faith and Tradition, brought about by the saving revelation of God in Christ, was confirmed by the consensus of the gathered representatives of the Church led by the Holy Spirit. [358]

Articles four and five classify the decrees into two categories. The first category is decisions regarding doctrinal problems such as the Trinitarian and Christological formulations, together with the Creed of Nicaea/Constantinople. These decrees formed the origins of both churches and shaped the language of their worship and prayers. The second is the canons of these councils which have been issued to establish a closer relation between faith and church

---

[358] Ibid.

life structure. They agree to differ regarding the authority of these canons which do not have the same authority as those addressing doctrinal issues. Article seven states two points of disagreement. The first is the addition of the filioque in the Lutheran Creed and the second is the receptions of the canons of the Nicaea II regarding iconoclasm and the veneration of the icons and images of the saints.[359]

There is a great difference between the Orthodox and the Lutheran Churches in the understanding of ecumenism. The Orthodox understanding of the ecumenism which was presented in New Delhi, shows that ecumenism means re-union with the Orthodox Church accepting its beliefs and doctrines as they are. This is exactly what happened in the dialogue between Jeremias II and the Lutherans in the sixteenth century. Consequently, Jeremais II invited the Lutheran to accept the Orthodox faith and to be part of the Orthodox Church. At the same level of invitation, the Lutherans did the same from the very beginning. The Lutheran started the dialogue by sending the *'Augsburg Confession'* re-titling it to be *'A confession of the Orthodox faith'*. Both invitation failed at that time, but the Orthodox Church understanding of ecumenism remains consistent to this day.. However, the Lutheran and Reformed churches understand ecumenism in terms of discussions between Christian denominations and do not insist that they alone are truly the church.

---

[359] Ibid.

Article five in the third plenary ends stating: 'Thus under the guidance of the Holy Spirit, divine revelation is living in the church through Holy Scripture and Holy Tradition'. This conceives Holy Scripture and Holy Tradition as two sources of revelation. This is a mistake since there is only one Source, which is the Holy Tradition. This has been corrected in the fourth plenary article two which ends: 'This "*euangelion*" of Jesus Christ, which by the operation of the Holy Spirit is communicated to us by the church to the end of the ages, is the holy Tradition'. The correction is clear where it called the whole '*euangelion*' of Jesus Christ as the Holy Tradition. Furthermore, article four in the same plenary defines the Holy Tradition as 'preserved, confessed and transmitted in scripture, in the lives of the saints in all ages, and in the conciliar tradition of the church.'

Both Churches agreed on the twenty-seven books the content of the New Testament, and thirty-nine books of the Old Testament. However, the ten (*deuterocanonical*) books of the Old Testament are varying in their authority. The Orthodox Church considered them as part of the Old Testament, while the Lutheran said only it is 'not rejected and profitable to read.'

The Lutherans have recognized that their own formula *sola scriptura* does not need to be inconsistent with the Orthodox view that Tradition is the total process of handing on divine revelation. This is a great step towards reciprocated understanding and encouragement to rely on *sola traditione* rather than *sola scriptura*.

Further meetings are needed to discuss other major points in the subject of the Holy Tradition. Such points will be detailed in the general conclusion.

6 GENERAL CONCLUSION

To conclude my discussion of the whole debate between *sola scriptura* from the Lutheran side and Tradition (including Scripture) from the Orthodox side, I will use three main sources: Gerhard Ebeling, a Lutheran Professor of Theology at Tübingen University; Father John Whiteford, a former Nazarene Pastor who converted to Orthodoxy; and finally, Professor Chrysostomos Konstantinidis, Metropolitan of Myra under the jurisdiction of the Ecumenical Patriarchate of Constantinople.

Ebeling, in his investigation of the interplay of *sola scriptura* with Tradition, asserts that the question and key point of this involvement is the terminology *sola scriptura*.[360] Astonishingly, he finds that this phrase is in question by the Protestant Churches. He says:

> The remark, credibly reported, from the Protestant side, in Ecumenical conversations, "*sola scriptura* has become obsolete", reveals a judgment based on insufficient grounds. One should be just as little swayed by this tendency as by the earlier

---
[360] Gerhard Ebeling *The Word Of God And Tradition: Historical studies Interpreting The Divisions Of Christianity*, (London: Collins, 1968), 102.

animosity towards the concept of Tradition. It would seem, however that the formula *sola scriptura* is in need of re-interpretation. Its genuine Reformation sense needs to be clarified in view of current misinterpretations, and an altered situation calls for a new response.[361]

However, John Whiteford argues that the assumptions of *sola scriptura* are false. He asks: If Protestantism and its foundational teaching of *sola scriptura* are of God, why did it result in over twenty-thousand differing groups that cannot agree on basic aspects of what the Bible says, or even what it means to be a Christian?

He discusses the three assumptions of *sola scriptura* and attempts to refute them. The first assumption is: The bible was intended to be that last word on faith, piety and worship. To explore this assumption he asks three sub-questions, the first is: does the Scripture teach that it is "all sufficient?" He finds out that those who believe in the sufficiency of the Scriptures uses (II Tim. 3:15-17) as their main argument to support their views. He avers that this was misinterpreted by the Reformers, as the word Scriptures in this verse does not mean at all the New Testament, Paul is speaking of the Old Testament, so if this passage is going to be used to determine the inspired authority it will exclude the entire New Testament and Tradition as well. Additionally, if Paul wanted to exclude Tradition why does he use in the same chapter (verse eight) the names of Jannes and Jambres, which are not in the Old

---

[361] Ibid, 102.

Testament but are found in Jewish Tradition. The second question is: What was the purpose of the New Testament Writings? He answers this question with an affirmation that the New Testament was not meant to provide a model for worship or any doctrine as a primary subject. Nevertheless the New Testament has four broad categories, gospels, historical narrative (Acts), epistles, and the apocalyptic book of Revelation. However the liturgical historians confirm that the early Christians continued to worship in a manner firmly based upon the patterns of Jewish worship, which was inherited from the Apostles. He avers that mistrusting the church in keeping and preserving apostolic worship, leads to the same mistrust in preserving the Scriptures. The third question is: Is the Bible, in practice, really "all sufficient for Protestants? He proves its insufficiency by asking many unanswered questions. He says:

> Why do Protestants write so many books on doctrine and the Christian life in general, if indeed all that is necessary is in the Bible? If the Bible by itself were sufficient for one to understand it, then why do not Protestants simply hand out Bibles? And if it is "all sufficient" why does it not produce consistent results, i.e. why do Protestant study Bibles, if all that is needed is the Bible itself? What is the purpose of the many Protestant study Bibles, if all that is needed is the Bible itself? Why do they hand out tracts and other materials? Why do they even teach and preach at all— why do not just read the bible to people? [...] Protestants instinctively know that the Bible cannot be understood alone. And in fact every Protestant

sect has its own body of traditions. [362]

The second assumption is: The Scriptures were the basis of the early Church, whereas Tradition is simply a "human corruption" that came much later. He argues that the church relied on the oral Tradition for four centuries before the final canonical form. He adds that Paul's words in (II Thess. 2:15) are clear evidence for such authenticated oral Tradition. He rejects the violent Protestant reaction against Tradition as a response to the flawed Roman Catholic concept of Tradition, which allowed growth and change from time to time. According to him the Orthodox Tradition does not grow or change, as the Truth does not change. He believes that the Latin West has corrupted the understanding of the nature of Tradition, while the true meaning is preserved in the Orthodox Church.[363]

The third assumption is: Anyone can interpret the Scriptures for himself or herself without the aid of the Church. This was claimed by the theologians at Tübingen in their dialogue with Jeremias II, but they confronted the Lutheran theologians with the claim that they used the interpretation of the Fathers only when it matched their opinions and they reject it when it opposed their teachings. In such case they gave their opinions more authority than the Fathers.[364]

---

[362] Whiteford, 8.
[363] Ibid, 9-13.
[364] Ibid, 13-14.

Ebeling discusses the reasons of the confrontation between Scripture and Tradition in a less vehement way than Whiteford. He states three reasons, first is: The common antithesis between *sola scriptura* and 'Scripture and Tradition'. Ebeling unearths the reason for this antithesis in the superficial consideration of the term "Tradition" and he recommends, for the ecumenical conversations, a need for corrections in the understanding of this term.[365] The second reason is: The significance of *sola scriptura* for the history of the concept of Tradition. He finds that the Medieval Church has "Scripture and Tradition" as an indivisible whole without question, but he argues the Patristic background in the actual discussions of this subject, especially in Irenaeus, Tertullian, Basil the Great and Vincent of Lérins, is in general scanty. He confirms that *sola scriptura* should not be separated from any theological problem when discussing Tradition.[366] The third reason is: The urgency of the problem of Tradition in Protestant theology. He finds that Tradition occupied a significant role in shaping the theological thought of Melanchthon and early Protestant theology in general. Here I think Ebeling is probably basing his conclusions on Fraenkel's *Testimonia patrum*. As I argue in the previous chapter, tradition is very important and even *necessary* from Melanchthon's point of view. Ebeling notices:

The chief Character of the historical approach is

---

[365] Ebeling, 102-103.
[366] Ibid, 104.

> its emancipation from the unproved assumption of the authority of Tradition. It is only when criticism enables us to see the process of transmission in its true perspective that we become aware of the powerful influence exerted by Tradition, and can realize more clearly the part which historically conditioned traditions have played in history. This has produced a greatly enhanced ability to understand the situation with regard to Tradition in detail, as well as basic insight into historical function of Tradition. [367]

He attests that the claim of the Protestant theologians to support *sola scriptura* and the claim of the Catholic theologians to write it off as obsolete makes him hesitate in assuming that the problem may be sorted out soon, and he recommends:

> It would, however, be a mistake to suppose that the problem of Tradition in the form in which it is presented by the historical approach of the new age, represents any confirmation of the Catholic conception of Tradition. The Catholic interpretation expressed in broad outline at the Councils of Trent and Vatican I is quite incapable of meeting the changed situation of the problem in the modern world. As the result of the new insight into the problem of historicity, both the Catholic doctrine of Scripture and Tradition, and the Reformers' principle of *sola scriptura*, needs fresh interpretation and clarification. The difficulties which the task involves have become apparent in the first place of Vatican II.[368]

Chrysostomos attributes the problem of the dichotomy of

---

[367] Ibid, 105.
[368] Ibid, 107.

Tradition to the Schism between East and West, but he insists that Orthodox Tradition is not one among many traditions but it is the One Holy Tradition of the Church of Christ himself, he says:

> This means that Tradition is "One" in principle, and "Undivided" as the revealed Truth; but it does not prevent us from speaking about some "traditions", which are met within the differentiated forms of the Church. This is the case of the Great Schism of the 11th century and has been multiplied in later centuries. The existence of one or more parallel traditions beside the one Tradition of the Church does not obscure or destroy the sacred character of the one Tradition; in the same way erroneous interpretations of the one revealed Truth do not destroy the Truth itself, but only damage the man who is misled by them.[369]

Chrysostomos asserts that the problem became wider after the Reformation and the dichotomy diverted into polytomy and the theme of the tradition took a broader meaning. The already deviating Western Tradition developed into new traditions under the weight of different theological and historical conceptions.[370] Such traditions are increasing and multiplied every day. They contain all the characteristics of the Reformers, their teachings, civilization and all other cultural aspects.[371] In spite of the Reformers' apparent rejection of the Western tradition, still every Reformed Church preserves or makes up its own traditions.

---

[369] Konstantinidis, 225-226.
[370] Ibid, 226.
[371] Ibid, 228.

Chrysostomos states:

> An anti-traditional system, depending one-sidedly on the Bible as Protestantism did, ignored Tradition. I will not examine the well-known thesis of Protestant theology on this subject. I think it is enough to say that Tradition is rejected as a source of revelation equivalent to Scripture. A first and common period of Tradition for Early Church is accepted, as a historical reality, but without any ecclesiastical authority. Though this is the theological conception of the Tradition in Protestantism, our subject, from the Historical point of view, can be presented as follows:
>
>> All forms of Protestantism, even the most liberal ones, have their own "tradition", some of which spring from their own bodies. I say "they have their own traditions," because no Church can be conceived to be without traditions.[372]

Ebeling in his analysis of the subject "*sola scriptura* and Tradition" points to some clear and common misunderstandings. The first is that *sola scriptura* is accused of hostility to Tradition. He asserts that the word of God itself reaches us in the form of Tradition and comments:

> For this purpose it would be better to adhere to the obvious meaning of Tradition: namely, that the gospel has reached us in the definite form of a history of which Jesus is the centre. Hence, since Jesus is its subject, the body of Tradition contained in both the New and the Old

---

[372] Ibid, 227.

Testament, is of unique and irreplaceable significance. Thus, *sola scriptura* clearly implies an adherence to the original Tradition, unmixed with foreign elements, permitting the force of the biblical Tradition to be transmitted to the modern world.[373]

The second is the priority and validity of Tradition as an objection against the *sola scriptura* principle. This objection was made to *sola scriptura* because of its restriction to the written word which implies disregard of the historical priority of oral transmission and the obvious fact that such transmission must have taken place through living witnesses. He re-understands *sola scriptura* of the Reformers and says:

> How remarkably deep was the Reformers' understanding of the Gospel is shown by the existence of this necessary connection between the content of this Tradition and its essential oral character. If, nevertheless, *sola scriptura* became the Reformers' watchword, this can only be understood in a sense that does not contradict the fact that the Word of God was imparted by verbal preaching, and was therefore oral Tradition. The exact value of *sola scriptura* is that it contributes to a right understanding of the essential oral character of 'transmission'. Hence it is only rightly understood when it is referred back to the event of preaching, and when the origin of Scripture is seen to lie in the act of preaching.[374]

The third is the formation of the Canon and its authority as an argument against *sola scriptura*. He admits that any attempt to prove

---

[373] Ebeling, 108-109.
[374] Ibid, 112.

sola scriptura from the Scripture is meaningless because it only proves the canonical authority of Scripture[375]. In addition to that, Whiteford argues that *sola scriptura* does not meet its own criteria and argues with the passages used by Reformers to prove it as explained earlier in this thesis as it contradicts II Thess. 2:15 and I Cor. 11:2.[376] Ebeling shows that all Protestant theologians in their doctrinal formulation confirm that canon and Church are inseparable which implies that Scripture and Tradition are inseparable. [377]

The third plenary of the Lutheran-Orthodox joint commission, which was discussed earlier in the fourth chapter of this thesis, accepted Tradition, but asked for more clear definition as to what is Orthodox. As article eight states "However, not every synod claiming to be orthodox, not every teaching of an ecclesiastical writer, not all rites are expressions of the holy Tradition, if they are not accepted by the whole church." In the same plenary (article eleven) the Orthodox understood the meaning intended by *sola scriptura* in terms of God's revelation and his saving acts through Christ in the power of the Holy Spirit, which means the Holy Tradition against all human traditions. In the other plenaries, they used the Fathers many times to explain and to clarify theological aspects as real witnesses to Holy Traditions.

---

[375] Ibid, 114-115.
[376] Whiteford, 14.
[377] Ebeling, 114.

Konstantinidis describes the various Protestant traditions as "consensus" of the illuminated individuals by the Holy Spirit in the Church with the presupposition that the presence of the Paraclete is tangible and assured.[378] Then he applies this principle on the Orthodox Tradition and states:

> Would not this "consensus" of the individuals be more positive and theologically more concentrated if accepted as a *"consensus Traditionis"*? And the Grace of Christ which assists and illuminates the individuals, can it be considered as the Grace which acts upon individuals as Fathers of the Church, and upon the Church itself, when it interprets and formulates its dogmas and its saving truth? Does not this accord of individuals have greater value than when it has the character of catholicity, antiquity and larger numerical agreement? On this point we need to bear in mind the definition of Tradition given by Saint Vincent of Lérins: *ab omnibus creditum est, hoc vere proprieque catholicum* (Vincent of Lérins, *Commonitorium*, 2, PL50, 640).[379]

Ebeling in his definition of the truth of *sola scriptura* asserts that a virtually unlimited extension of the authoritative canons was the foundation of the Reformation debate about Tradition. This absurd extension results from the unclear nature of the Catholic conception of Tradition.[380] On the other hand, Whiteford stresses that Orthodox Tradition begins from Adam and stretches through time to all Church members forever. Furthermore, he says that

---

[378] Konstantinidis, 228-229.
[379] Konstantinidis, 229.
[380] Ebeling, 123.

Protestantism protested against the papal abuses, which did not exist prior to the breaking between the East and the Roman West.[381]

Looking to the third plenary again with optimistic eyes we find good progress in understanding each other. However, the call for "Retraditioning" by Konstantinidis is in more vital need today in order to have any real progress in the ecumenical conversations. This shows more understanding and awareness of the problems and the solution from Konstantinidis side rather than Whiteford. Konstantinidis declares:

> "Retraditioning!" Let us finish this paper by this term. Please do not consider it either too bold or too unusual. My protestant brothers will agree with me that the period from the beginning of the Reformation until now was a period of "detraditioning" in spite of some notions of "traditions" which they have cultivated from time to time. They will also agree that this period of detraditioning was negative for ecclesiological restoration. We have already said: Church and Tradition are bound together. If we now take into consideration that with the delay of ecclesiological restoration, any desire and attempt for reunion must remain unfruitful, we can understand, I think, what is meant by "Retraditioning". We cannot consider ecclesiological restoration and reunion except as a sincere effort for "Retraditioning." [382]

From the beginning the Church believed in one source of

---

[381] Whiteford, 23.
[382] Konstantinidis, 230.

revelation, which was the Tradition. After the Great Schism the West developed the two sources theory and the tension started to arise between Tradition and Scripture as two different sources. This tension paved the way for the Reformers to pit Scripture against Tradition. In other words, to pit Tradition I against Tradition II and to adopt the principle of *sola scriptura*. The modern discussions proved that *sola scriptura* is obsolete or at least misunderstood and now it is time for *sola traditione*. The joint commission had achieved some progress and it is recorded in the plenaries. For Lutherans, to accept that the whole *"euangelion"* of Jesus Christ is Tradition is a great step towards mutual understanding. But it burdens both the Orthodox Church and the Lutherans to start to work towards this deeper understanding of *sola traditione*.

One of the major convergences after that was the content of the Scripture. Both Churches agreed on the New Testament content. They agree on thirty-nine books of the Old Testament, but still the ten deuterocanonical books have varied authority in both churches. Further meetings are needed to state an agreed authority for these books. Another point of convergence was the authority of the seven ecumenical councils. This was accepted in the plenaries except the seventh council. Additional discussions have to clarify the decrees of the other first six councils one by one to be in full agreement.

The next major conflict to be discussed is the priesthood.

The Lutherans believe in the general priesthood of all believers. They appoint a minister to perform the sacraments. On the other hand, the Orthodox Church believes in the general priesthood of all believers in addition to the special priesthood for the clergy to perform the sacraments. Sorting out this problem will help in all other sacramental problems.

The number of sacraments is debatable between both churches. It needs an extensive discussion as it is considered the main sources for the means of Grace in the Orthodox Church.

Fr. John Meyendorff identifies a distinction between "Tradition" and "traditions" as one of the major needs of the current ecumenical dialogue, and one of the most pressing tasks for Orthodox theologians.[383] He adds that this is needed not only for the ecumenical dialogues, but also for "a number of reformist movements inside the Orthodox world itself"[384]. He confirms that in modern times the dialogues have taken a new pragmatic direction. They put aside all the human traditions and local customs and examine the matters that have doctrinal implications. He quotes Patriarch Anthimos in his reply to encyclical *Praeclara gratulationis* (1895) of Pope Leo XIII where he affirms that the unity of faith can be achieved without the unification of "the order of

---

[383] Meyendorff, 21.
[384] Ibid, 22.

the holy services, hymns, liturgical vestments and other similar things which, even when they preserve their former variety, do not endanger the essence and unity of the faith."[385]

However, there are still some similarities between the current problem between the Orthodox Church and the Catholic Church as existed during the Reformation. Anthimos declares that only the matters which have doctrinal implications should be investigated and he excludes some customs and traditions. Nevertheless, Orthodox theologians need to work more towards a full list of customs and tradition which could be acceptable locally within the Church. Additionally, they have to clarify what parts of "Tradition" which are essential for salvation.

Konstantinidis and the Orthodox-Lutheran joint commission call on the Orthodox to do some examination of their own approach. As the Orthodox have still not really given a full and clear answer to the question raised at the very beginning: how does one distinguish between Tradition and traditions? What are the criteria? Konstantinidis thus calls on Orthodox and Lutherans to engage, together, in the joint task of sorting this question out or, at least, trying to reach a better understanding of it. The criteria for determining the Holy Tradition are of great importance. The Orthodox Church has to draw the line between the customs and the Traditions. Only in this way, I would think, could the

---

[385] I. Karmires, *Ta dogmatika kai symblika mnemeia tes orthodoxou katholikes ekklesias*, vol. II (Athens, 1953), 935 quoted in Meyendorff, 25.

Lutherans genuinely accept *'sola traditione'* approach. In other words, the Lutheran Church has to re-tradition, i.e. to rely on *sola traditione* rather than *sola scriptura*.

BIBLIOGRAPHY

The Ante-Nicene Fathers Series. Edinburgh: T&T Clark, reprint 1996.

The Nicene and Post-Nicene Fathers, First Series. Edinburgh: T&T Clark, reprint 1996.

The Nicene and Post-Nicene Fathers, Second Series. Edinburgh: T&T Clark, reprint 1996.

Luther, Martin, *55- Volume American Edition Luther's Works*, ed. Jaroslav Pelikan and Helmut T. Lehmann. [CD-ROM]. USA: Fortress Press and Concordia Publishing House, 2001.

Didache, or Teaching of the Twelve Apostles. Trans. by Roberts Donaldson. Available [Internet] <http://www.earlychristianwritings.com/text/didache-roberts.html> [3rd March 2004].

Letter of Clement To The Corinthians, trans. by Roberts Donaldson. Available [Internet] < http://www.earlychristianwritings.com/text/1clement-roberts.html> [3rd March 2004].

Cyril of Jerusalem, Catechetical Lectures, 4: 21. Available [Internet] <http://www.ccel.org/fathers2/NPNF2-07/Npnf2-07-09.htm#P452_92480> [14th March].

Augustine, The Enchiridion, 30. Available [Intenet] <http://www.iclnet.org/pub/resources/text/ipb-e/epl-01/agenc-02.txt> [14th March 2004].

Augustine, Letter 82.1, See *Sant'Agostino, Epistolae. Available* [Internet]<http://www.sant-agostino.it/latino/lettere/index2.htm> [9 June 2004].

Luther on The bondage of the Will. Available [Internet] <http://www.covenanter.org/Luther/Bondage/Bowexord.ht

m> [18March 2004].

Letter (28) from Augustine to Jerome. Available [Internet] <http://www.newadvent.org/fathers/1102028.htm> [19March 2004].

Luther, The Smalcald Articles, On Human Tradition. Available [Internet] <http://www.iclnet.org/pub/resources/text/wittenberg/concord/web/smc-03o.html> [23 March 2004].

The Council of Trent, the Fourth Session. Available [Internet] <http://history.hanover.edu/texts/trent/ct04.html> on [6th December 2004].

Luther M., *An Address to the Christian Nobility of the German Nation.* Available [Internet] <http://www.iclnet.org/pub/resources/text/wittenberg/luther/web/nblty-03.html> [6th December, 2004].

Gregory Nazianzen, *"On the Holy Sprit".* Available online <http://www.ccel.org/fathers2/NPNF2-07/Npnf2-07-46.htm#P4606_1453815> [3rd December, 2004].

Bruce, F. *Tradition Old and New.* Exeter Devon: The Paternoster Press, 1970.

Clapsis, E. *Orthodoxy in Conversation: Orthodox Ecumenical Engagements*, Brookline: Holy Cross Orthodox Press, 2000.

Deansely, M. *A History of the Medieval Church 590- 1500.* London: Methuen & Co. Ltd., 1925.

Debis, G. "The Concept of Tradition In The Fathers Of The Church", *Greek Orthodox Theological Churches Review*, 15, no.1 (Spring ,1970): 22-55.

Douglas, J.D. *The New International Dictionary of the Christian Church.* Exeter: The Paternoster Press, 1974.

Ebeling, G. *The Word Of God And Tradition, Historical studies Interpreting The Divisions Of Christianity.* London: Collins,1968.

Ehrman, B. *The New Testament: A Historical Introduction To The Early Christian Writings*. New York, Oxford: Oxford University Press, reprint 1997.

Erickson John, Bird Thomas, ed. *Vladimir Lossky: In the Image and Likeness of God*. London & Oxford: Mowbrays, 1974.

Florovsky, G. *Bible, Church, Tradition: An Eastern Orthodox View*, in Richard Haugh eds. *Volume One in The Collected Works of George Florovsky*, Vaduz, Europe: Büchervertriebsanstalt, 1987.

_____ *Collected Works of Georges Florovsky, Vol. II, Christianity and Culture*. Belmont MA: Norland publishing, 1974.

_____ *The Orthodox Church and The Ecumenical Movement Prior to 1910*, in *A History Of The Ecumenitcal Movement. Vol.1*, eds. Ruth Rouse and Stephen Charles Neil, London :SPCK,1986.

Fraenkel, P. *Testimonia Patrum: The Function of The Patristic Argument In The Theology Of Philip Melanchthon*. Geneve: Librairie E. Droz, 1961.

Gibbon, E. *The History of The Decline and Fall of The Roman Empire*, [CD-ROM]Vol. 4, USA: Albany, 1997.

Hendrix, S. "Deparentifying the Fathers: The Reformers and Patristic Authority." In *Tradition and Authority in the Reformation*, ed. L. Grane, A. Schindler and M. Wried, Asgate: Variorum, 1996: 55-68.

_____ "*We are all Hussites? Huss and Luther revisited*". *Archiv für Reformationsgeschichte 65*. (1974): 134-161.

Herbon, J. *Huss and His Followers*. London: Geoffrey Bles, 1926.

Hughes, P. *A History of the Church to the Eve of the Reformation*. London: Sheed and Ward: reprint 1976.

Konstaninidis, C. *The Significance Of The Eastern And Western*

Traditions Within Christendom, in *The Orthodox Church In Ecumenical Movement*. Geneva: World Council of Churches, 1978.

Lohse, B. eds. and trans. by Roy Harrisville, *Martin Luther's Theology: Its Historical and Systematic Development*. Edinburgh: T&T Clark, 1999.

Malaty, T. *The Orthodox Concept: Tradition and Orthodoxy*. Sporting, Alexandria: St. George Church, 1979.

Meijering, E. *Melanchthon And Patristic Thought, The Doctrine OF Christ and Grace, The Trinity And The Creation*. Leiden: E.J Brill, 1983.

Meyendorff, J. *Living Tradition*. Crestwood, NY: St. Vladimir's Seminary Press, 1978.

Oberman, H. *The Dawn of the Reformation: Essays in Late Medieval and Early Reformation thought*. Edinburgh: T& T. Clark, 1986.

_____ *The Harvest of Medieval Theology, Gabriel Biel and Late Medieval Nominalism*. Cambridge, Massachusetts: Harvard University Press, 1963.

_____ *Forerunners of the Reformation, The shape of late Medieval Thought Illustrated by Key Documents*. Philadelphia: Fortress Press, 1982.

Patelos, G. *The Orthodox Church in the Ecumenical Movement, Documents and Statement*. 1902-1975. Geneva: World Council of Churches, 1978.

Pelikan, J. *Obedient Rebel: Catholic Substance and Protestant Principle in Luther's Reformation*. London: SCM Press, 1964.

Schaff, P. *History of The Christian Church*, 8 v., 1:431 [CD- ROM] : The Master Christian Library, Version 6, Ages Software digital Library, USA: Albany, 1998.

Scouteris, P. "The Orthodox Understanding of Tradition", *Sobornost - Eastern Churches Review*, Vol.4, No. 1982: 30-37.

Sproul, R. and James Boice, eds. *The Foundation of Biblical Authority*. London, Glasgow: Pickering & Inglis,1978.

Ware, T. *The Orthodox Church*. England :Penguin Books,1983.

Ware, K. *How Are We Saved? The Understanding of Salvation in the Orthodox Tradition*. Minneapolis, Minnesota: Light and Life publishing, 1996.

Werckmeister, J. "The Reception of The Church Fathers In Canon Law," In *The Reception of the Church Fathers in the West, From Carolingians to The Maurists*. Irena Backus, eds., 53-82, 2 v., Leiden: E.J. Brill, 1997.

Yeago, D. "The Catholic Luther", *First Things: A Journal of Religion and Public Life*, 61 (March 1996): 37-41.

Zernov, N. Eastern Christendom: A Study of the Origin and Developments of the Eastern Church, London: Weilden and Nicolson, 1961.

G. Debis, *Tradition in the Orthodox Church*. Available [Internet] <http://www.goarch.org/ourfaith/articles7116.asp> [9th October 2002].

M. Aghiorgoussis, *The Dogmatic Tradition of the Orthodox Church*. Available [Internet] <http://paul.goarch.org/en/ourfaith/articles/article8038.asp> [2nd October 2002].

Whiteford J, *Sola Scripture, In The Vanity Of Their Minds*. Available [Internet] <http://orthodoxinfo.com/inquirers/tca_solascriptura.htm> [25th November 2003].

Icons of Macedonia: Beginnings- The Iconoclasts versus the Cult of Icons. Available [Internet] < http://www.soros.org.mk/konkurs/019/eng/txt01.htm>[14th March 2004].

George Tavard Biography. Available [Internet] <http://www.assumption.edu/brighton/tavard/english/biography.htm>[May 5th 2004].

In Memoriam : Heiko Augsutinus Oberman (1930-2001). Available [Internet] <http://info-center.ccit.arizona.edu/~dlmrs/DH09,2.html > [5th May 2004].

John Erickson, *Jaroslav Pelikan: The Living Legend in our Midst.* Available [Internet] <http://www.svots.edu/Events/Summer-Institute/2003/readings/Pelikan-Legend.html > [24 March 2004]

Tibbs E., *16th Century Lutheran & Orthodox Exchange, Patriarch Jeremias II, The Tübingen Lutherans, and the Greek Version of the Augsburg Confession: A Sixteenth Century Encounter, Fuller Theological Seminary*, 2000. Available [Internet] <http://www.stpaulsirvine.org/html/lutherna.htm > [16th May 2002].

The Official web site of LWT. Available [Internet] <http://www.lutheranworld.org/What_We_Do/OEA/Bilateral_Relations/OEA-Lutheran-Orthodox.html> [20th December 2003].

Lutheran- Orthodox Joint commission, Available [Internet] <http://www.helsinki.fi/~risaarin/lutortjointtext.html> [20th December,2003].

Yeago, D. "The Catholic Luther". *First Things: A Journal of Religion and Public life*, 61 (March 1996):37-41. Available [Internet] <http://www.firstthings.com/ftissues/ft9603/articles/yeago.html> [12th June 2003].

ABOUT THE AUTHOR

V. REV. FR. MARK AZIZ is a Parish Priest at St. Mark Coptic Orthodox Church in Scotland. He holds a Master of Theology degree from the University of Aberdeen in Scotland. Fr. Mark is working on his doctoral research at Trinity College. He is an author and a prominent lecturer on Patristic and dogmatic theology, Biblical Counseling, the Holy Tradition, history of the Reformation and the Orthodox View on various contemporary topics.

www.ingramcontent.com/pod-product-compliance
Lightning Source LLC
Chambersburg PA
CBHW071917290426
44110CB00013B/1393